RAND HEALTH

T0303092

The Unified Behavioral Health Center for Military Veterans and Their Families

Documenting Structure, Process, and Outcomes of Care

Nicole K. Eberhart, Michael Stephen Dunbar, Olena Bogdan, Lea Xenakis, Eric R. Pedersen, Terri Tanielian

Sponsored by the New York State Health Foundation

For more information on this publication, visit www.rand.org/t/RR1647

Library of Congress Cataloging-in-Publication Data
is available for this publication.

ISBN: 978-0-8330-9688-3

Published by the RAND Corporation, Santa Monica, Calif.

Preface

Addressing the behavioral health needs of veterans and their families is a national priority. Over the past decade, multiple programs both within and outside of the federal government have been implemented to build additional capacity and expand access to high-quality behavioral health care for veterans and their families. Much of the nongovernmental effort has been funded by private philanthropy in an effort to build and expand public-private partnerships with the Department of Veterans Affairs.

In 2012, Northwell Health, a private-sector, nonprofit health system, and the Northport Veterans Affairs Medical Center launched the Unified Behavioral Health Center for Military Veterans and Their Families. This unique clinic, located in Bay Shore, New York, provides behavioral health services for both veterans and their family members. In 2014, the RAND Corporation was asked to design and conduct an evaluation of this model to document its structure, process, and outcomes of care in an effort to inform potential replications of this approach. This report presents the findings from this evaluation.

This evaluation was sponsored by the New York State Health Foundation and conducted within RAND Health. A profile of RAND Health, abstracts of its publication, and ordering information can be found at www.rand.org/health.

Contents

Figures and Tables

Figures

Tables

Summary

Background

Many veterans and their families struggle with behavioral health problems, family reintegration difficulties, and relationship problems. Yet veterans and their families face barriers to receiving adequate care for these problems. Notably, although many veterans are eligible to receive care at Department of Veterans Affairs (VA) facilities, family members are not eligible and therefore must seek care elsewhere. This situation can pose a barrier to family members' access to care and also make it more difficult for veterans and families to receive high-quality services that are coordinated and integrated across providers.

Will a new model of care that colocates and coordinates behavioral health services for veterans and their families address these barriers? This report presents an evaluation of one instance of such a model, the Unified Behavioral Health Center (UBHC) for Military Veterans and Their Families. The UBHC, located in New York state (NYS), is a public-private partnership between the Northwell Health System and the Northport Veterans Affairs Medical Center (VAMC) that is providing colocated and coordinated care with the goal of improving behavioral health care for veterans and their families. There is evidence that NYS veterans have unmet behavioral health needs. NYS has the fourth-highest number of resident veterans nationwide (U.S. Department of Defense [DoD], 2010), and there is evidence that NYS veterans and their families are at risk for behavioral health problems and in need of services (see, e.g., Vaughan et al., 2011). While more than one-half of NYS veterans could likely benefit from some type of behavioral health care, a study found that only about one-third actually received behavioral health services, and of those receiving services, only one-half received minimally adequate care (Schell and Tanielian, 2011). In addition, nearly one-half of spouses reported difficulties dealing with their partners' behavioral health issues, and one-third reported concerns regarding veteran's reintegration into the daily family routine. Spouses of veterans in NYS also reported depression and limited engagement in behavioral health services.

Purpose and Approach

The public-private partnership model embodied in the UBHC is an innovative approach to expanding services for veterans and their families. To foster understanding of the UBHC model and shed light on how it is serving veterans and their families, RAND evaluated the center's activities. The evaluation was intended to document the implementation of a unique public-private collaborative approach for providing care to veterans and their families, in order to assess the approach's viability, identify implementation challenges and successes that the program can learn from, and facilitate its replication in other communities should it prove successful. This report presents the results of RAND's evaluation.

The evaluation addressed four questions:

- What resources and capacities were available for providing care in the UBHC?
- What barriers and facilitators to implementing this model of care did the center encounter?
- What services were delivered, and what were the characteristics of the patients who received these services?
- How did receiving care affect patients' health outcomes?

The evaluation had two components. The first component focused on documenting the structures of care (the capacities and resources that the center developed and employed—e.g., facilities, staff, technology, infrastructure) and the processes of care (the services delivered—

e.g., individual psychotherapy, medication management—and who received them). The second component focused on outcomes of care. These outcomes refer to the measures of functioning and symptoms that patients experience as a result of the types of care they received—in other words, measuring the improvements in health that the processes are intended to produce. For the first component, the evaluation used data from site visits and focus groups, as well as administrative data. For the second, it used patient-reported outcome data that were collected and shared by UBHC staff.

Key Findings

Capacity for Care

- The UBHC treated its first patient in late 2012, after approximately five months of construction. As of July 2016, the center is up and running and delivering a range of behavioral health services to veterans and their families (e.g., individual and group psychotherapy, family therapy, medication management).
- The center colocates and coordinates care across two independently governed sides: One side, the VA Clinic at Bay Shore, a community-based outpatient clinic, is operated by the VA; the other side, the Mildred and Frank Feinberg Division, is operated by Northwell Health, a private-sector provider. The two sides have two different managing authorities, sets of procedures, and reporting requirements. One side serves veterans, while the other side is available to service members, veterans, and their families but primarily serves family members. Each side has separate entrances, information systems, and processes for monitoring performance.
- The partnership between the Feinberg Division and the VA Clinic at Bay Shore sides of the UBHC allows for convenient access to behavioral health services for veterans and family members and facilitates exchange of information between the different sides of the center, which can improve coordination of care. The information exchange occurs primarily through team meetings, other in-person contacts, and the phone. These communication mecha-

nisms are effective in the context of a relatively small center, but communication "infrastructure" would likely have to be enhanced for a larger program to be successful (see the "Recommendations for Improving or Replicating the UBHC Model" section).

Barriers to Implementation and Service Delivery

- Gaining senior level buy-in from the local VAMC and VA Central Office took time but was ultimately achieved by focusing on the potential benefits of the program for veterans and their families.
- Coordinating the construction of a new facility that met the needs of both Northwell Health and the Northport VAMC was challenging because of numerous regulatory considerations, some of which were not clear up front.
- The funding model used in the first three years is likely not sustainable. The Feinberg Division provided services at no charge, generating no revenue. This is likely not a sustainable funding model because it relies on donations and philanthropic support to pay for operating expenses. Recognizing this, Northwell Health has been working toward developing more-sustainable funding for the Feinberg Division throughout the UBHC's implementation and recently implemented a new billing system. Programs seeking to replicate the UBHC model may benefit from designing and implementing a sustainable funding plan from the initiation of the program.
- There is an absence of institutionalized and codified procedures for collaborative activities (e.g., a liaison between sides of the center), and these may present future challenges. VA Clinic at Bay Shore staff noted that there is currently no directive in the VA to implement these kinds of programs and services, and the staff expressed a desire for clear directives that would support integration and collaboration and ensure that current effective strategies are preserved in the event of staffing changes.

Facilitators of Implementation and Service Delivery

- Staff at both Northwell Health and the Northport VAMC championed and facilitated the establishment of the UBHC. Since its

establishment, staff within both systems have forged strong working relationships.
- A Robert Wood Johnson Foundation grant was a critical catalyst in the establishment of the center.
- Media attention helped to advertise the availability and services offered by the center.
- The UBHC staff reported taking special pride in one achievement in particular: This was as one provider described it, "the healing that has occurred" as a result of being able to serve veteran families through providing collaborative care.

Services Delivered

- The two sides of the center had different patterns of service utilization: The VA Clinic at Bay Shore provided fewer services to a larger number of individuals, while the Feinberg Division provided more-intensive services to a smaller number of individuals. As a result, the overall number of patient encounters was comparable across the two sides of the UBHC, despite very different patient loads.
- Both sides, however, succeeded in becoming operational and delivering a substantial amount of services (more than 7,000 behavioral health encounters on each side of the center) in a relatively short time frame (three years). This was notable considering that it was a new center ramping up its capacity to provide care (e.g., through staffing) and reaching out to potential patients in the community for the first time.

Patient Outcomes

- UBHC patients consistently expressed satisfaction with their experiences at the center and the care they received, according to our interviews and a satisfaction survey. Family members we spoke with remarked that the UBHC "is a place for families to go that is familiar with veterans' issues." Beyond the advantage of having providers who understand the issues that veteran families face, patients recognized the advantages of the family receiving

coordinated care; for instance, one patient noted that "when [providers] communicate, it's fantastic."
- Adult patients treated on the Feinberg Division side of the UBHC showed improvement in key outcomes, including symptoms of depression and posttraumatic stress disorder, family functioning, and quality of life. Child patients displayed fewer behavioral health problems.

Recommendations for Improving or Replicating the UBHC Model

Institutionalize and Codify the Practices That Are Working

The UBHC has established strategies, policies, and procedures designed to enhance the collaborative effort. However, some of these practices have not been institutionalized. For example, there is currently a VA staff member informally acting as a liaison to coordinate care between the two sides of the center; although this coordination is conducted effectively, the liaison role could be formalized to ensure that strong communication between organizations continues. More broadly, the VA Clinic at Bay Shore should consider formally protecting the time that their providers spend collaborating, because this is time not spent in direct patient care or other administrative duties.

Facilitate Easier and Closer Collaboration by Enhancing Communication "Infrastructure"

Collaboration would be further enhanced if staff could integrate treatment plans across the center's two sides and could more easily communicate with each other. The organization of the physical space can also enhance communication.

Integrate treatment plans. Collaboration would be enhanced by use of integrated treatment plans that staff on both sides of the center contribute to and can readily access.

Share access to patient records. The collaboration would also be enhanced by providers on both sides of the center having easy access to each other's patient records, so that it is easier to track the care a patient is receiving from other providers.

Provide secure email. It would also be helpful if providers could securely email each other; currently, they cannot include patient names in email communications, so communicating about a shared patient requires a phone call or in-person consultation. The organizations could also consider developing new platforms for secure electronic communication between different IT systems.

Enhanced communication infrastructure that facilitates less burdensome data collection, monitoring, and sharing is critical to supporting partnerships between the VA and private organizations, particularly when they are scaled beyond a single relatively small program.

Create a Physical Space That Is Conducive to Collaboration and Family Friendly

The clinic space should be organized in a manner that facilitates clinical staff's efforts to coordinate care; the current organization, with a shared conference room and kitchen and easy staff access between the sides of the center, achieves this goal. Staff could consider organizing the clinic in such a way that the collaboration is readily apparent to patients, if this is desired. A single entrance, single reception, and uniform decor would communicate to patients that this is a collaborative center rather than two distinct entities. Regardless of the extent to which spaces are shared across organizations, there should be close communication regarding the establishment and construction of the physical space from the start of the process. Because the UBHC and other sites seek to provide services to family members of veterans, including children, it will be important to ensure that these spaces appear not only veteran friendly but also family friendly.

Ensure Adequate Capacity (Staffing and Space) to Meet Patient Needs

The UBHC may benefit from an expansion in both staffing and physical space, if patient interest in the center continues to grow. In particular, increased staff at the VA Clinic at Bay Shore would ensure that there is availability to serve veterans who have family members receiving services on the Feinberg Division side of the UBHC. Increasing the *overall* capacity of the VA Clinic at Bay Shore through increasing staff hours there (e.g. more full-time staff instead of part-time staff) would ensure that the VA Clinic at Bay Shore has adequate capacity to serve veterans participating in the collaboration, without affecting capacity to serve veterans whose families do not receive care on the Feinberg Division side of the center.

Provide a Continuum of Evidence-Based Services

As more settings work to serve veterans and their families experiencing behavioral health problems, it will be important not only to ensure the provision of evidence-based interventions but also to provide a continuum of services, including prevention (e.g., psychoeducation and other programs), in addition to referrals to other types of support (e.g., financial and legal support, other family support services). For both prevention and treatment services, community-based organizations and clinical settings should adopt a systematic approach for selecting, training, delivering, supervising, and monitoring the fidelity of evidence-based practices relevant to the population. Systematic use of evidence-based practices could ensure the effectiveness of treatment, provided that training is also systematic and that the interventions are delivered with fidelity. In selecting evidence-based approaches, organizations wishing to replicate the UBHC model may want to focus on time-limited (i.e., short-term) approaches and techniques or services that require lower-level (i.e., less expensive) staff to increase capacity and reduce costs.

Prioritize Outcome Monitoring and Quality Improvement for the Center as a Whole

The UBHC and other similar centers should carefully and routinely reevaluate their battery of measures to choose the ones that are least burdensome to patients and most helpful for informing clinical decisionmaking and outcome monitoring. To increase the integration and coordination of services, as well as to enable better tracking of patient outcomes over time, we recommend that the entire UBHC (both the VA Clinic at Bay Shore and Feinberg Division sides) implement the same set of patient-reported outcome measures to inform patient care and enable ongoing quality-improvement efforts across all partnering entities. For example, if families who received some care from both sides of the UBHC completed the same set of measures, it would facilitate setting and tracking higher-order, family-system–level treatment goals. Consistent measurement across the entire UBHC would also facilitate program monitoring and evaluation.

Conclusions

Overall, the UBHC has successfully implemented a promising public-private partnership model for providing behavioral health care for veterans and their families in the same facility. Providers coordinated efforts to deliver high-quality care, the center geared up to deliver a range of therapeutic services for a large number of patients in a relatively short time, patients were happy with the services they received, and their symptoms and functioning improved significantly over time.

Providing colocated and coordinated care can potentially address barriers to care for veterans and their families. Although many veterans are eligible for VA services, most veterans' families are not, leading different members of families to seek care in different settings, with no easy way to exchange information and coordinate care between VA providers and family members' providers (see Pedersen et al., 2015, for a review). The UBHC addresses this barrier by providing care that is colocated and coordinated.

The UBHC provides care that is oriented toward the needs of veteran families. Family members we spoke with expressed that the UBHC plays a vital role in their communities, citing that, in their experience, providers not affiliated with the VA are insensitive to the impact of posttraumatic stress disorder and other special issues facing the families of veterans. Family members we interviewed saw the UBHC as a unique place where military families could receive care and be understood. UBHC staff and patients alike touted the advantages of coordinated care in which the different providers treating a family are in close communication with one another; all interviewees felt that this coordination greatly improved the quality of care that family members received. Patients expressed high levels of satisfaction with the care they received.

Although the model has been successfully implemented, with strong preliminary outcomes, there are areas that could be improved as the UBHC continues to grow and develop. While staff and patients were happy with the collaborative relationships between providers, collaboration could still be closer than it currently is. Staff members regularly have to circumvent various challenges to collaboration.

Other partnerships between local VAMCs and private health systems that want to accomplish similar objectives can learn from the UBHC launch and implementation. In addition to the issues related to barriers to collaboration and the lack of codified practices, there were barriers to establishing the center that other programs may be able to circumvent. Building the center was a complicated process, but many of the barriers the UBHC faced could potentially be avoided by having close communication between the private organization and the appropriate VA staff through all phases of establishing the center, with key players at the table from the start. Another potential barrier for other potential partnerships is cost. However, initial expenses could be reduced by using an existing facility rather than building a new one. Further, ongoing expenses could be reduced by billing patients from the start and potentially using less expensive staff (e.g., fewer members of the psychiatry staff, greater use of interns) and providing less expensive care (e.g., less individual therapy and more groups; however, this may not be feasible for small centers).

Our evaluation suggests that, overall, the model has been successfully implemented by the UBHC and has great potential to be helpful to the veteran families it serves.

Acknowledgments

We are grateful to many individuals for their contributions to this project. We would like to thank Deborah Scharf for playing a key role in the evaluation design and Bing Han for his statistical consultation. We express our gratitude to staff at the Unified Behavioral Health Center, Northwell Health, and the Northport Veterans Affairs Medical Center for assisting us with the evaluation by participating in interviews and providing data. Lastly, we thank our reviewers, Patricia Lester and Lisa Meredith.

Support for this work was provided by the New York State Health Foundation (NYSHealth). The mission of NYSHealth is to expand health insurance coverage, increase access to high-quality health care services, and improve public and community health. The views presented here are those of the authors and not necessarily those of NYSHealth or its directors, officers, and staff.

CHAPTER ONE

Background

Many veterans and their families struggle with behavioral health problems, family reintegration difficulties, and relationship problems. Substantial barriers prevent veterans and their families from receiving adequate care. Notably, although many veterans are eligible to receive care at Department of Veterans Affairs (VA) facilities, family members are generally not eligible for VA care and must seek their health care elsewhere. This situation can pose a barrier to family members' access to care and also make it more difficult for veterans and their family members who do get care to receive services that are coordinated across providers. Will a new model of care that provides colocated and coordinated behavioral health services for veterans and their families address these barriers? This report presents an evaluation of one instance of such a model, the Unified Behavioral Health Center (UBHC) for Military Veterans and Their Families.

Addressing the Behavioral Health Needs of Veterans and Their Families Is a National Priority

Veterans and Their Families Struggle with Behavioral Health Concerns

Approximately one-fifth of the approximately 2.8 million veterans of the conflicts in Iraq and Afghanistan are struggling with behavioral health concerns, such as posttraumatic stress disorder (PTSD), traumatic brain injury (TBI), depression, and substance use disorders (Ramchand et al., 2014; Schell and Marshall, 2008; Seal et al., 2011).

Despite rates of behavioral health concerns higher than the civilian public, less than 50 percent of veterans in need of services actually seek care (Bray and Hourani, 2007; Gorman et al., 2011; Pietrzak, Johnson, et al., 2009; Schell and Marshall, 2008). Veterans and their spouses collectively report substantial family reintegration difficulties, reduced marital quality, and increased rates of separation and divorce compared with nonmilitary families (Riviere et al., 2012; Sayers et al., 2009). In addition to dealing with the behavioral health issues of their veteran partners, military spouses themselves experience high rates of behavioral health concerns, such as depression and anxiety (Eaton et al., 2008; Mansfield, Kaufman, Marshall, et al., 2010).

Children exposed to parental wartime deployment also suffer from family relational problems and behavioral health concerns, such as depression and conduct problems (Gorman, Eide, and Hisle-Gorman, 2010; Jordan et al., 1992; Lester et al., 2010; Mansfield, Kaufman, Engel, and Gaynes, 2011; McFarlane, 2009). For example, researchers have noted increases in documented behavioral disorders in medical charts during periods of parental deployment (Gorman, Eide, and Hisle-Gorman, 2010), and test scores at school have been shown to decrease during periods of parental deployment (Engel, Hyams, and Scott, 2006). In addition, it may not be deployment itself that only explains problems for children; rather, deployment may affect parental behavioral health problems, which then have a direct relationship with such outcomes as parenting challenges, impaired parent-child relationships, and overall functioning of the family. For example, parental PTSD attributed to trauma experienced while deployed was associated with parenting challenges among Army National Guard fathers (Gewirtz et al., 2010). Spouses of deployed service members reported declines in parenting satisfaction during deployments (Meadows, Tanielian, and Karney, 2016). Moreover, the higher levels of self-reported parental stress and overall perceived psychological stress by nondeployed parents have been shown to be associated with children's poorer psychological functioning (e.g., behavioral problems, attention problems) (Flake et al., 2009). Combined, these factors all can negatively affect the family unit and present challenges for children.

Veterans and Their Family Members Face Barriers to Receiving Adequate Care

Nearly one-half of veterans and their spouses have reported logistical barriers that precluded them from receiving care, including perceived high costs of behavioral health care, difficulty getting child care or time off work, not knowing where to receive such care, not knowing what affordable care options are available, and concerns related to the beliefs that others would view them negatively for seeking such care (Eaton et al., 2008; Hoge et al., 2004; Pietrzak, Johnson, et al., 2009; Schell and Marshall, 2008; Vaughan et al., 2011). Also, while nearly all recent veterans are eligible for medical and behavioral health care at the VA (e.g., free care for the first five years postdeployment), in most instances, family members are not eligible for this care. Consequently, veterans and their families have to learn to navigate two separate systems of care (i.e., the VA and another hospital or clinic) to achieve and maintain family well-being. This dual-system navigation can be a formidable task: Exchange of information between VA providers and family members' providers can be time-consuming and strain already limited resources in trying to coordinate care between two separate clinics. Also, family members may be unaware of their care options after leaving the military health system and TRICARE. For example, in qualitative work, RAND researchers found that veterans and their spouses are generally unaware of their affordable care options (Schell and Tanielian, 2011). As another example, in a large study of military and veteran caregivers, RAND also found that approximately one-third of post-9/11 caregivers did not have a regular source of health care and that one-quarter lacked health insurance (Ramchand et al., 2014). Veterans themselves recommended expanded and accessible VA services for the family members of veterans, such as support programs and access to the same quality care that veterans receive (Farmer et al., 2011). While some family members, including those enrolled in the VA's comprehensive post-9/11 caregiver support program, can receive medical care from the VA, the size and scope of their care utilization is unknown.

New Policies Address the Concerns About Unmet Behavioral Health Needs

In August 2012, President Barack Obama signed an executive order to improve the behavioral health care of veterans, service members, and their families. Efforts to achieve these goals have included increasing capacity for health care at the Veterans Health Administration (VHA), promoting research on the development and dissemination of effective treatments, and promoting suicide-prevention efforts (U.S. Department of Defense [DoD], VA, and U.S. Department of Health and Human Services, 2013; Office of the Press Secretary, White House, 2012). The executive order also called for collaboration between the VHA and the Department of Health and Human Services to identify local community partners to improve access to care for services for veterans in the community. Recently, the Office of the Chairman of the Joint Chiefs of Staff also called for more public-private partnerships to target the health and wellness needs of veterans as the conflicts in Iraq and Afghanistan end (Office of Warrior and Family Support, Office of the Chairman of the Joint Chiefs of Staff, 2013). Public-private partnerships have been a focus of the VA's Veterans Policy Research Agenda as well, which specifically calls for more research to evaluate and monitor public-private partnerships, to inform best practices for defining and measuring success, and to help develop innovative platforms for enhancing communication between veterans, family members, and caregivers about services available through partners of the VA (Office of Policy and Planning, VA, 2014). The VA's strategic plan for fiscal years 2014–2020 also aims to "enhance and develop trusted partnerships," and to "enhance VA's partnerships with federal, state, private sector, academic affiliates, veteran service organizations, and non-profit organizations" (Office of Policy and Planning, VA, 2014). Thus, the strategy promotes public-private partnerships as a potential solution to address the gaps between veterans' needs and the availability of services—particularly behavioral health services.

A New Model Exists for Colocating and Coordinating Care for Veterans and Their Families in New York State

One such public-private partnership has emerged in New York state (NYS); this partnership is the first to test its potential for improving behavioral health care for veterans and their families. There is evidence that NYS veterans have unmet behavioral health needs. NYS has the fourth-highest number of resident veterans nationwide (DoD, 2010), and there is evidence that NYS veterans and their families are at risk for behavioral health problems and in need of services. For example, in a large survey of NYS veterans and their spouses, researchers found concerning rates of probable PTSD (16 percent), depression (16 percent), and past-month binge drinking (38 percent) (Vaughan et al., 2011). While more than one-half of NYS veterans could likely benefit from some type of behavioral health care, a study found that only about one-third actually received behavioral health services; of those receiving services, only one-half received minimally adequate care (Schell and Tanielian, 2011). In addition, nearly one-half of spouses reported difficulties dealing with their partners' behavioral health issues, and one-third reported concerns regarding veteran's reintegration into the daily family routine. Spouses of veterans in NYS also reported depression (10 percent) and limited engagement in behavioral health services (i.e., 21 percent received past-year services; 14 percent desired services but did not initiate treatment). In short, policymakers and providers must do more to improve the health of NYS veterans and their families.

To address the behavioral health care barriers experienced by NYS veterans and their families, Northwell Health Systems, a private-sector, nonprofit health system, and the Northport Veterans Affairs Medical Center (VAMC) collaborated to create the UBHC for Military Veterans and Their Families—a unique community-based behavioral health center for military veterans and their families. This collaboration is specifically designed to overcome access and coordination barriers to care by housing behavioral health care for veterans and their families within the same facility. The approach is intended to allow veterans and their families to receive the same behavioral health care within one setting, increase communication between veterans' and their families' providers, help coordinate care for veterans and their family members in both family-based and individually based approaches, allow for easier and streamlined information exchange between providers, reduce the stigma of seeking care by including family members in specialized care of such disorders as PTSD, and increase military cultural competency among the non-VA providers. The center demonstrates a public-private collaborative model of care that may be broadly applicable beyond NYS and across other VA facilities partnering private health care systems.

Purpose of This Report

The public-private partnership model embodied in the UBHC reflects an innovative approach for expanding services for veterans and their families. However, little has been documented about how the center came to fruition and whether it is meeting its stated objectives. To foster greater understanding of the UBHC model and shed light on how it is serving veterans and their families, RAND conducted an evaluation to assess this public-private collaboration to expand access to behavioral health services for veterans and their families. The evaluation was intended to document the implementation of a unique public-private collaborative approach for providing care to veterans and their families, in order to assess the approach's viability, identify implementation challenges and successes that the program can learn from, and facilitate its replication in other communities should it prove successful.

The evaluation addressed four research questions:

- What resources and capacities were available for providing care in the UBHC?
- What barriers and facilitators to implementing this model of care did the center encounter?
- What services were delivered, and what were the characteristics of the patients who received these services?
- How did receiving care affect patients' health outcomes?

Organization of This Report

The remainder of this report is organized as follows: Chapter Two describes our research methods. Chapter Three presents information gathered about the development and current structure of the UBHC. Chapter Four presents descriptive results about the center's processes of care, as well as information about patient characteristics. Chapter Five presents results about patient outcomes. Chapter Six documents the lessons learned and presents our recommendations and conclusions.

CHAPTER TWO

Evaluating the Unified Behavioral Health Center for Military Veterans and Their Families: Methodological Approach

The evaluation had two main components. The first focused on documenting the *structures* of care (the capacities and resources that were developed and employed [e.g., staff, technology, infrastructure]) and describing the *processes* of care (the intervention activities that were delivered and who received them [e.g., clinical services administered]). Our team designed the evaluation using a structure-process-outcomes framework (see Figure 2.1; Donabedian, 1966, 1980). Structures of care refer to those structural aspects that help to define capacity; this includes the physical structure (size, layout), as well as the staff (type, capabilities, size) and the resources staff members have available to deliver services (e.g., clinical tools, such as health information technology [IT]). The process of care includes those types of services or procedures that are used to address a particular health problem. In the case of the UBHC, the process includes the types of therapeutic services that are offered and used (e.g., individual psychotherapy, medication management) by providers to address behavioral health issues among the patient population.

The second component focused on assessing *outcomes* of care. These refer to the measures of functioning and symptoms that patients experience as a result of the types of care they received—the improvements in health that the processes are intended to produce (e.g., improvement in behavioral health symptoms and quality of life). All methods were reviewed and approved by the RAND Human Sub-

Figure 2.1
Structure-Process-Outcomes Framework

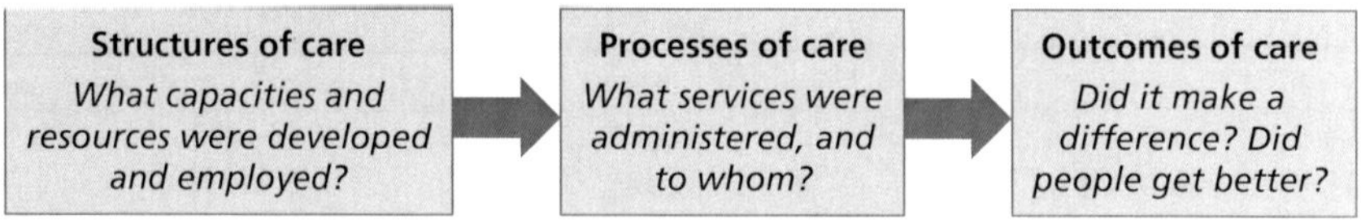

RAND *RR1647-2.1*

jects Protection Committee. Northwell Health's and the Northport VAMC's institutional review boards (IRBs) reviewed the methods as well and concluded that the project was program evaluation and not research and thus not subject to IRB review. A data use agreement for a limited data set and a confidentiality agreement were used to access patient-level data from Northwell Health, and a memorandum of understanding (MOU) with the Northport VAMC allowed us to conduct the evaluation.

Documenting Center Structure and Processes of Care

Effective delivery of care involves multiple organizational features operating across both structural and process levels. To understand these features, we employed multiple methods and used various data sources to allow a comprehensive assessment of the structures and processes associated with care delivery at the UBHC. These methods included primary data collection from stakeholders (i.e., through site visits, staff interviews, and patient focus groups), review of reports to the center's sponsor, review of administrative records, and examination of service utilization data. The UBHC is essentially made up of two physical parts, the VA Clinic at Bay Shore, a community-based outpatient clinic (CBOC)—literally on one side of the building—and a privately funded veteran and family clinic on the other. These two sides are managed separately, and, as a result, we talk about our procedures for gathering and assessing information about both "sides" of the UBHC. How these two sides work together will be discussed in Chapter Four, but it is important to understand how our methods varied across the two different sides.

Site Visit and Focus Groups

Two members of the evaluation team visited the UBHC and conducted semistructured interviews with administrators involved in the development or management of the center, administrative support staff, behavioral health providers, and patients.

The team interviewed all behavioral health staff and key administrators from both Northwell Health and the VA Clinic at Bay Shore sides of the center. The Northwell Health side is referred to as the Mildred and Frank Feinberg Division (Feinberg Division). Staff interviews were conducted individually or in small groups. Interview groups did not combine Feinberg Division and VA Clinic at Bay Shore staff and did not combine clinical and administrative staff (i.e., groups contained only staff from the same organization and same level of authority). We conducted phone interviews after the site visit with staff who were not available during the visit and followed up with some administrators by phone or email as needed to clarify responses.

We conducted two focus groups with patients of the UBHC, one consisting of veterans (N = 6, all male) and another consisting of family members of veterans (N = 9, all female). All focus group participants were 18 years or older and were currently receiving care from the UBHC. No focus groups were conducted with child patients or nonpatient family members or collaterals.

The evaluation team also toured the UBHC to understand the unique aspects and key physical features of the collaborative center.

Interview participants were asked about their involvement and experiences with the UBHC. Interview protocols were guided by key publications about the integration of public-private partnerships and the provision of adequate care for veterans and their families (Pedersen et al., 2015; Suter et al., 2009; Tanielian et al., 2014). Interviews focused on the history and goals of the center; implementation; governance; shared structures; systems; and culture, integration, and facilitators and barriers. Interviews were semistructured to allow for responses to prompt follow-up questions for further understanding or clarification. Separate interview protocols were developed for patients (veterans and family members), staff and administrators, and leadership. Interviews lasted 30–60 minutes and were documented in notes taken by RAND staff. Protocols and questions were developed using a matrix of key topics for each focus group or individual interview (see Table 2.1). RAND staff reviewed notes from the interviewers and organized responses by key area and themes that were identified through group discussion and consensus within the evaluation team. First, we

Table 2.1
Key Topics Covered in Interviews and Focus Groups

Topic	Administrator Interviews	Clinician Interviews	Patient Focus Groups
Background	X		
Structure of the center	X		
Nature of partnership	X		
Population served	X		
Planning and implementation	X		
Goals	X		
Budget/finances	X		
Daily operations	X	X	
Services offered	X	X	
Care coordination/cross collaboration/integration culture	X	X	
Policies and procedures	X	X	
Services offered	X	X	
Performance management and evaluation			
Barriers and challenges	X	X	X
Successes	X	X	X
Access to care	X		X
Care experience			X

linked the protocol questions by interviewee with the appropriate key topic. Next, we inserted interview notes into the key-topic framework by topic, and interview data were reviewed by the principal investigator and the project associate. The key topics suggested some a priori themes, and themes were identified through review of interview notes that highlighted the unique attributes of the UBHC. Two team members individually studied the raw data organized by outlined topic and provided comments and further subtopics based on participant and client responses. Finally, we summarized the raw data by topic and subtopic to create a coherent story of the UBHC's implementation and operation.

Review of Administrative Reports

We reviewed semiannual and annual narratives that the UBHC provided to one of its sponsors, the Robert Wood Johnson Foundation (RWJF). Reports detailed progress on key objectives at six-month intervals and highlighted the impact the center had on patients, staff changes, and patient flow (see North Shore-LIJ Health System, 2013, 2014, 2015). In addition to documenting progress, the reports allowed the UBHC to provide input on barriers and issues that may require assistance from the funding partnership staff. As relevant and appropriate, we incorporated information from the narratives into this report.

Service Utilization Data

To understand who was receiving care and the types of care that were delivered, we requested data on the size and characteristics of the patient populations served on both sides of the UBHC. The type and level of detail of these data differed depending on the side of the center. We received deidentified individual-level data using a secure data-transfer protocol from the Feinberg Division (i.e., age, gender, race and ethnicity, education, employment status, income, military service, treatment history, diagnosis, services received) and conducted descriptive analyses to summarize patient characteristics and service utilization. For patients seen on the VA Clinic at Bay Shore side of the UBHC, a VA data analyst on-site provided us with aggregate-level data for patients with behavioral health issues.

Assessing Outcomes of Care

To understand how services received at the UBHC affected the outcomes of those served, we requested access to patient-reported outcomes data that had been collected by UBHC staff. The Feinberg Division side of the center serves both child and adult patients and routinely collects data on individuals treated in the clinic to monitor patient outcomes in response to treatment and augment treatment planning. Clinic staff administer a variety of assessment measures of symptomatology and functioning at three-month intervals. The battery of measures was chosen at the time of Northwell Health's RWJF application, and the specific measures administered to a given patient were selected by Feinberg Division clinicians according to what they believed was most appropriate for the patient based on the initial intake assessment (patient outcomes were consistently assessed at three-month intervals, but only families and couples were routinely administered family and couple measures, only those presenting with PTSD symptoms were routinely assessed with regard to PTSD symptomatology, and so on). The VA Clinic at Bay Shore does not routinely and consistently collect patient-reported outcomes, but it does implement VA-mandated standard screenings (e.g., for suicide risk, depression, TBI, PTSD, alcohol abuse) for patients. However, individual-level data from these screenings were not available to RAND.

Because of resource constraints, the current evaluation relied on available previously collected outcome data; thus, outcome data are only available for patients treated on the Feinberg Division side of the UBHC. Similarly, there are no comparison data from a control group of individuals who did not receive care at the UBHC.

Patient-Reported Outcome Measures: Adults

Feinberg Division staff administered several measures of depression, anxiety, and PTSD-related symptomatology as well as family and relationship functioning and overall quality of life satisfaction to adults every three months. The following subsections discuss the specific measures.

Beck Depression Inventory II

The Beck Depression Inventory II (BDI-II) is a widely used 21-item inventory measuring the severity of depression in adolescents and adults (Beck, Steer, and Brown, 1996). Scores range from 0 to 63, with validated clinical cut-off points (e.g., scores 0–13 are interpreted as "minimal" symptoms; scores above 28 correspond to "severe" depressive symptoms). The scale has been shown to have good internal consistency (Cronbach's alpha = 0.91; Dozois, Dobson, and Ahnberg, 1998), and there are numerous studies that provide evidence for the scale's reliability and validity across a range of populations (e.g., Dozois, Dobson, and Ahnberg, 1998); Osman et al. (2004) found good reliability and validity when testing the BDI-II with adolescent psychiatric patients.

Beck Anxiety Inventory

The Beck Anxiety Inventory (BAI) is a 21-item inventory using a rating scale from 0 to 3 to assess anxiety levels in adolescents and adults (Beck and Steer, 1993). Similar to the BDI-II, scores range from 0 to 63, and guidelines for score interpretation are provided (e.g., scores greater than 29 are interpreted as "severe" anxiety symptoms). The measure age range is 17–80, but the measure has been used in peer-reviewed studies with adolescents ages 12 and older. There is strong evidence for the measure's reliability and validity (e.g., good internal consistency, with Cronbach's alpha equaling 0.92 to 0.94; see Beck et al., 1988; Fydrich, Dowdall, and Chambless, 1992).

Family Assessment Device

The Family Assessment Device (FAD) is based on the McMaster Model of Family Functioning (MMFF) and measures structural, organization, and transactional characteristics of families. The FAD assesses six dimensions of the MMFF—affective involvement, affective responsiveness, behavioral control, communication, problem-solving, and roles. The current evaluation examined the general family functioning scale, an overall measure of family functioning (Epstein, Baldwin, and Bishop, 1983). Higher scores indicate poorer levels of family functioning. The FAD has shown acceptable psychometric properties (Bihum et al., 2002; Miller et al., 1985). The general-family functioning scale has shown good internal consistency (Cronbach's alpha ranges from

0.83 to 0.86; Kabacoff et al., 1990) across nonclinical, psychiatric, and medical populations.

Dyadic Adjustment Scale

The Dyadic Adjustment Scale (DAS) is a self-report measure of relationship quality (Spanier, 1976). It is a 32-item measure with four subscales (dyadic consensus, dyadic satisfaction, dyadic cohesion, and affectional expression) developed for married couples or similar dyads. Items have varying response scales, and higher scores on each scale indicate higher levels of relationship quality. It has been acknowledged as one of the best paper-and-pencil indicators of dyadic adjustment (Cohen, 1985; Jacobson and Follette, 1985; Johnson and Greenberg, 1985). The DAS shows high internal consistency (Cronbach's alpha = 0.96; Spanier, 1976; Sharpley and Cross, 1982), and there is strong evidence for its reliability and validity (Carey et al., 1993; Graham, Liu, and Jeziorski, 2006).

Quality of Life Enjoyment and Satisfaction Questionnaire–Short Form

The Quality of Life Enjoyment and Satisfaction Questionnaire–Short Form (Q-LES-Q–SF) assesses the degree of enjoyment and satisfaction experienced by individuals in various areas of daily functioning (Endicott et al., 1993). Scores range from 14 to 70 and are interpreted as a percentage of the maximum possible score, with higher percentages indicating better quality of life. The measure shows good internal consistency (Cronbach's alpha = 0.90; Stevanovic, 2011), is reliable and valid among clinical populations (Ritsner et al., 2005; Mick et al., 2008; Stevanovic, 2011), and has been used to assess quality of life among veteran populations (Pietrzak, Tsai, et al., 2015).

PCL-5—PTSD Checklist for DSM-5

The Posttraumatic Stress Disorder Checklist for DSM-5 (PCL-5) is a 20-item measure that assesses the 20 *Diagnostic and Statistical Manual of Mental Disorders*, fifth edition (DSM-5), symptoms of PTSD (Weathers et al., 2013). The PCL-5 is used for monitoring symptom change during and after treatment, screening individuals for PTSD, and making a conditional PTSD diagnosis. Items are scored from 0 to

4, with higher total symptom scores indicating greater symptom severity (total scores above 33 may indicate clinically significant symptoms; Weathers et al., 2013). The Posttraumatic Stress Disorder Checklist (PCL) was revised to reflect DSM-5 changes to the PTSD criteria, and changes in existing and new symptoms are reflected in the PCL-5. There is evidence that the measure has strong internal consistency (Cronbach's alpha = 0.94; Blevins et al., 2015), strong reliability, and strong validity (Blevins et al., 2015; Liu et al., 2014).

Outcome Measures for Children

Feinberg Division providers routinely assessed behavioral health outcomes in child patients (i.e., younger than 18 years old) via two measures—one that relied on parent reports of child behaviors and one that relied on youth self-reports of behavioral health.

Child Behavior Checklist for Ages 6–18

The Child Behavior Checklist for Ages 6–18 (CBCL/6–18) is a standardized measure completed by the parent or caretaker who spends the most time with the child (Achenbach and Rescorla, 2001). It provides ratings for ten competence and 120 problem items corresponding to the Youth Self Report (YSR). Scores are typically transformed and interpreted as T-scores relative to the standardized sample. The items cover physical problems, concerns, and strengths, and scales have been shown to have good internal consistency (Cronbach's alphas ranging from 0.71 to 0.89; Nakamura et al., 2009). An examination of a large clinical sample of children and adolescents found the measure to be reliable and valid (Nakamura et al., 2009).

Youth Self Report

The YSR is a self-administered survey developed by Thomas Achenbach and derived from the CBCL (Achenbach, 1991). The YSR assesses the emotional and behavioral problems in adolescents. The total scale score has been shown to have good internal consistency in both younger and older youth (Cronbach's alphas for both younger and older youth were 0.93; Ebesutani et al., 2011), and the measure is reliable and valid (Ebesutani et al., 2011; Izutsu et al., 2005).

Statistical Analysis of Outcome Measures

The effect of treatment on patients' symptoms and functioning over time was analyzed overall as well as at three-month intervals over the course of treatment (up to one year) using Stata/SE 13.1 statistical analysis software. The 12-month observation period allows for examination of trajectories of symptom change over time and is a period of observation often used to assess intervention effects in clinical trials (see, e.g., Katon et al., 2001; Miklowitz et al., 2007; Miranda et al., 2003). To estimate both the individual fixed effects across patients and random effects within patients, as well as to maximize the ability to use as much available data as possible, the treatment effect was modeled using mixed-effects models of repeated-measures data.

The primary outcome for the analysis was severity of depression symptoms, as measured by BDI-II. Secondary outcomes included the BAI, the FAD, the DAS, the Q-LES-Q–SF, the PCL-5, the CBCL, and the YSR.

Most of the outcomes of interest were modeled on the individual level, while joint family questionnaires (the FAD and the DAS), as well as the CBCL, were modeled on both individual and family levels. Based on statistical judgment (parameter estimates testing in multivariate modeling, as well as such model specifications tests as Akaike information criterion, Bayesian information criterion, and likelihood-ratio test) and medical judgment (understanding of factors associated with a specific outcome), predictors were selected for the final multivariate repeated-measures mixed model. For all adult outcomes, the model predictors included demographic characteristics (age, gender, ethnicity), level of education, and family income, as well as military status (active duty, reserves, veteran, military child, military family member, military spouse, other close relationship). The child outcomes (the CBCL, the YSR) had a smaller set of controls because of insufficient numbers of observations in their specific cases: Models for the CBCL controlled for gender only, and those for the YSR controlled for age, gender, and ethnicity.

Using the final repeated measures mixed effects model specification, each clinical outcome was analyzed in two ways. First, the *mean treatment effect* was estimated based on the linear growth model using continuous time. Then, the clinical outcomes were analyzed at each separate time of their repeated measurements to estimate the *treatment effect relative to baseline* at each subsequent three-month assessment (three months, six months, nine months, and 12 months) since initiating treatment. The results of both models are reported for all outcomes.

CHAPTER THREE

The Center's Creation and Capacity for Care

This chapter describes the origins of the UBHC and its structure—its physical setting, infrastructure, staff resources, and operational procedures. The chapter also presents our assessment of the center's capacity for delivering care.

Origins of the Unified Behavioral Health Center

The UBHC for Military Veterans and Their Families, located in Bay Shore, New York, in Suffolk County on Long Island, opened in 2012. The facility provides behavioral health care for veterans and their families and represents a formal collaboration between Northwell Health (formerly the North Shore Long Island Jewish Health System) and the Northport VAMC. Each of these systems is described briefly below. The timeline for key events for establishing the UBHC is shown in Figure 3.1.

Northwell Health

Northwell Health is an integrated health system, based in Great Neck, New York, in Nassau County on Long Island, with 21 hospitals and more than 61,000 employees. The rebranding of the organization in January 2016—from North Shore Long Island Jewish Health System to Northwell Health—reflects Northwell's expansion beyond Long Island to the broader New York metropolitan area, as well as an increasing organizational emphasis on overall wellness. Part of Northwell's mission is improving the health of the neighborhoods it serves,

Figure 3.1
Timeline of Key Events for Establishing Center

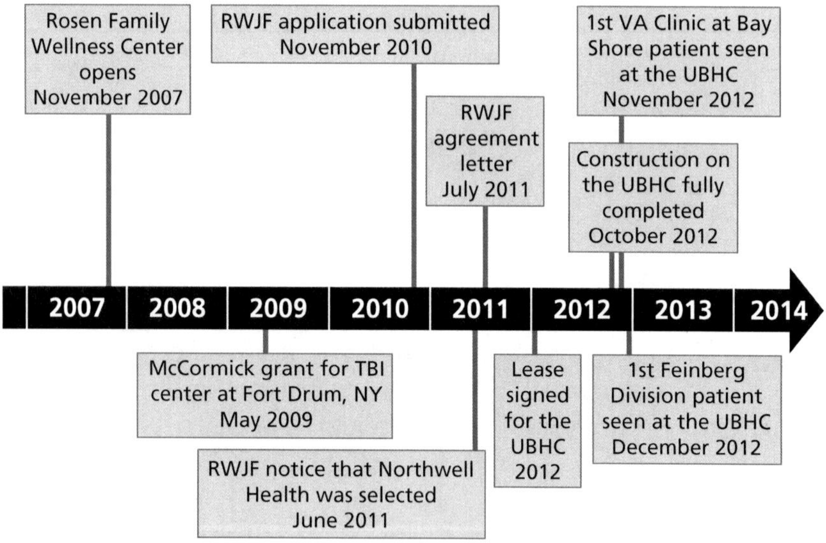

RAND *RR1647-3.1*

and this includes a long-standing commitment to providing care to military veterans and their families. Suffolk and Nassau counties alone have a combined veteran population of 125,000 (National Center for Veterans Analysis and Statistics, VA, undated).

Northwell Health has a history of providing services to veterans and their families. In 2007, with funding from the Rosen Family and Federal Law Enforcement Foundation, Northwell psychiatrists and other physicians, psychologists, and social workers began providing free, confidential behavioral health care services to veterans and their family members through the Florence and Robert A. Rosen Family Wellness Center (the Rosen Center), located in Nassau County. In 2009, Northwell Health established the Office of Military and Veteran's Liaison Services as a health and wellness resource center. This office oversees and coordinates programs, such as the community-based Rosen Family Wellness Center, dedicated to the needs of veterans and their families.

Northwell Health also provides care for individuals with TBI. In 2009, Northwell Health obtained a Robert R. McCormick Foundation grant to fund a TBI center serving veterans at the Fort Drum, New York, military installation. Northwell's McCormick grant also funded a part-time neuropsychologist fellow to assist the Northport VAMC with new federally mandated TBI evaluations for veterans returning from Operations Enduring Freedom and Iraqi Freedom. In addition, Northwell Health provided services to veterans on Long Island at Zucker Hillside Hospital in Queens.

Northport VAMC

The VA operates the largest integrated health care system in the world. VA facilities (hospitals, clinics, vet centers, and domiciliaries) are organized into a series of 21 Veterans Integrated Service Networks (VISNs). The VA facilities within NYS are split between VISN 2 and 3. VISN 3 includes all of the VA facilities around New York City and on Long Island, as well as New Jersey. Within VISN 3, there are eight medical centers, three domiciliaries, ten veteran centers, and more than 30 community-based outpatient clinics. The Northport VAMC, one of the medical centers within VISN 3, provides medical, surgical, psychiatric, rehabilitative, and skilled nursing care to veterans living on Long Island. Veterans can also receive services through the Northport VAMC at any one of its five CBOCs on Long Island (see Figure 3.2). In total, the Northport VAMC served 31,534 patients last year.

Taking Advantage of an Opportunity

As part of ongoing efforts to improve and expand services for veterans and their families, Northwell Health staff reported that they had long recognized the potential value of a partnership with the VA. While staff at the Northport VAMC indicated that they shared Northwell Health's concern for military and veteran families, the VA's mission is to serve veterans, and it has only limited authority to serve some veteran spouses and children. Thus, the idea for a unified clinic to serve veter-

Figure 3.2
Location of the UBHC

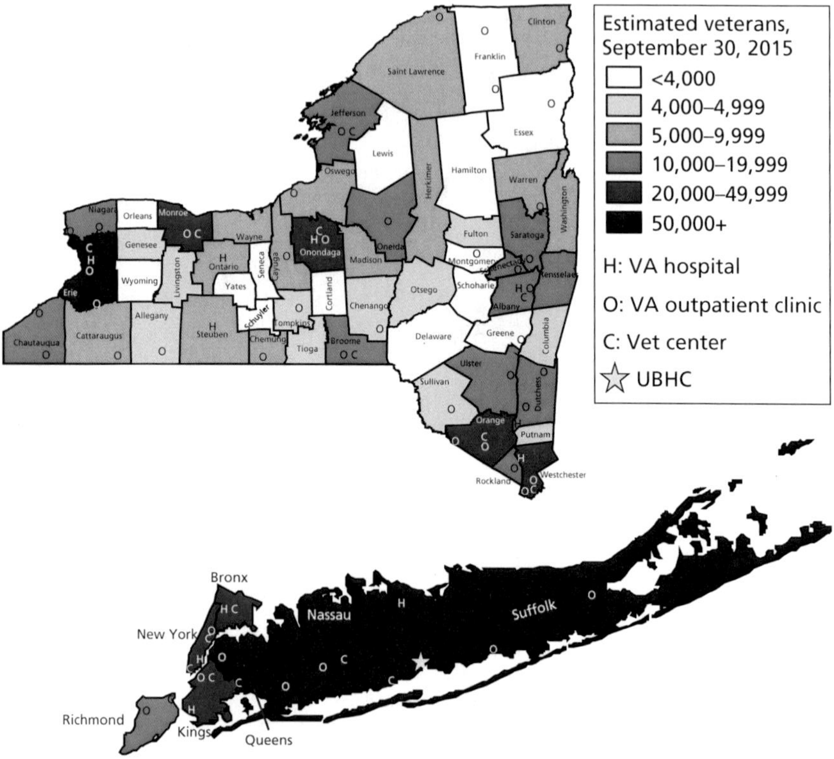

RAND *RR1647-3.2*

ans and their families was not necessarily intuitive. Two developments, however, combined to pave the way for the current collaboration.

In the fall of 2010, Northwell Health applied for a grant from the RWJF's Local Funding Partnerships initiative, a national program designed to support community-based projects that improve health care for vulnerable populations, to support the UBHC. According to Northwell Health staff, veterans receiving care at the Rosen Center did not like receiving care at the VA, and the Northwell Health team saw this as an opportunity to create a partnership with the VA that would allow veterans to seek care in a different environment. To help foster the relationship between Northwell Health and the VA, Northwell Health hired a veteran to act as an Office of Military and Veterans Liaison Services manager.

At the same time that Northwell Health was exploring ways to expand services for veterans and their family members with the RWJF grant, staff at the Northport VAMC reported that the VA found itself needing to close two antiquated CBOCs in Bay Shore, Long Island, and to open a single new CBOC in their place. When Northwell Health was able to provide the VA with a building to house a new CBOC in Bay Shore, interview participants reported that the idea of a unified behavioral health center for veterans and their families became a reality. The UBHC, which opened its doors in late 2012, enabled the Northport VAMC to collaborate with Northwell Health in addressing a shared concern—the behavioral health of current military personnel, veterans not eligible for the VA, and their family members.

The overarching mission of the UBHC is to improve the behavioral health and well-being of military veterans and their spouses, partners, and children by providing behavioral health services in a common setting. The specific goals of the UBHC are to increase access to services, reduce symptoms and improve quality of life, reduce stigma through family-focused care and outreach, demonstrate the viability of public-private collaboration, and promote replicability. The specific issues that the UBHC team evaluates and treats include long-term exposure to stressful or traumatic events, fear for the safety of loved ones, PTSD, anxiety, depression, family conflicts, and children's behavioral problems.

Formalizing the Partnership

To outline the relationship and parameters for the partnership, an MOU was established between the Northport VAMC and Northwell Health at the UBHC. It should be noted, however, that the UBHC was open for about a year before the MOU was officially in place. According to those we interviewed, the original vision of the UBHC was an equal partnership, in which both sides could actively promote themselves, endorse each other, and make direct referrals. After the UBHC opened, however, VA staff learned that direct referrals were not allowed because of federal regulations; instead, VA staff were obliged to refer the Feinberg Division side of the UBHC operated by Northwell Health along with all the other relevant referrals in the region. If they did mention the Feinberg Division as an option, they needed to state that the UBHC was a "collaboration" and not a "partnership" (North Shore-LIJ Health System, 2013).

UBHC staff reported that the Northport VAMC made multiple attempts to obtain an MOU that would have the purpose of allowing them to preferentially refer to the Feinberg Division side of the UBHC. According to them, obtaining approval for the MOU took about a year and required multiple revisions by legal counsel on behalf of both the VA and Northwell Health. At present, the MOU is in place, and the VA side of the center can preferentially refer patients to the Feinberg Division side, operated by Northwell Health.

Establishing the Center: Funding, Approvals, and Construction

Northwell Health staff reported that their vision of a unified behavioral health center for veterans and their families grew out of experiences with the Rosen Family Wellness Center, which first opened in November 2007. Northwell Health leadership reached out to Northport VAMC leadership regarding collaborating on the center. UBHC staff reported that obtaining buy-in from VA leadership was challenging and time-consuming, as described in more detail in the sections on barriers and facilitators.

To support the operation of the UBHC, Northwell Health received a grant for $300,000 from RWJF in July 2011. As a condition of the grant, Northwell Health had to provide 100-percent matching funds, but it was able to raise more funding than required, so the Northwell Health matching contribution actually exceeded this amount. Northwell Health staff reported that the total annual operating expenses for their side of the UBHC have ranged from around $500,000, when the clinic had recently opened and staffing levels were lower, to more than $670,000 in 2015, after staffing levels were gradually increased. Table 3.1 summarizes Northwell Health's annual operating expenses for the UBHC. It should be noted that the VA covers the expenses for its staff working at the VA Clinic at Bay Shore and does not incur any special expenses to support the UBHC collaboration because it uses

Table 3.1
Feinberg Division Operating Budget

Expense	2013 ($)	2014 ($)	2015 ($)
Staffing expenses—salary and fringe	317,861	428,116	507,896
Other expenses (e.g., communications/marketing, travel, rent/tax, consultants)	184,149	171,821	162,565
Total salary and other expenses	502,009	599,937	670,462

NOTE: These expenses have been rounded to the nearest dollar.

existing staff and resources and operates the VA's side of the center like any other CBOC.

The grant and matching funds were designated for clinic operating expenses and did not cover the costs of renovating a new facility, which were approximately $1 million (inclusive of construction, equipment, and furnishings). Northwell Health did extensive fundraising to acquire the money needed to open and operate the center. Specifically, the funds were raised for the Military Veteran Program at Northwell Health and were then distributed to the UBHC and the Rosen Center.

Northwell Health secured a ten-year lease to the building, but the building needed extensive renovation before it could house the UBHC. Northwell Health took the lead on developing the site, in consultation with VA staff. The construction took approximately five months to complete. Building the shared facility required a lot of coordination with not only the contractors but also several program and regulatory officials because of the unique needs of each collaborating organization. According to those in charge of executing the building renovation, in the initial scoping of the project, it was not clear how exactly staff from the two organizations would interact, what physical areas would be shared, and how shared areas would be accessed.

Northwell Health staff in charge of the renovation reported that, in addition to clinical considerations related to how providers from the two organizations would share the facility and use the space to facilitate patient care, there were also numerous regulatory considerations, some of which were not clear up front. In particular, Northwell

Health staff reported that, as a federal entity, the VA had very specific requirements for its buildings, guiding everything from the positioning of outlets to the types of lightbulbs used. Northwell Health staff reported that shortly before the building was scheduled to open, VA staff expressed concerns about security issues (i.e., the need for panic buttons and emergency locks in offices), the conference room, and the ramp used for accessible building entry—which was compliant with Americans with Disabilities Act standards but not the VA's standards, which are different. According to those interviewed, another issue that arose was how to keep each organization's IT infrastructure private and secure. There was only one room for IT equipment in the renovated space, but it was not acceptable to each organization that the other could access it. To maintain separation and security, the pieces of IT equipment from each organization are in separate locked cabinets within the room.

The first veteran patient to receive care at the UBHC did so in November 2012, and the first veteran family member to receive care at the UBHC did so the following month.

Structural Capacity

The physical setting, infrastructure, staff resources, and operational procedures of the UBHC are integral to its capacity to deliver care to patients. These are described below.

Location and Setting

The UBHC facility is located in downtown Bay Shore, on Long Island. The building is nestled within a series of commercial-use properties, all of which share a rear parking lot. The UBHC building can be accessed through a single door, but upon entering the vestibule, visitors have to choose between entering one of two doors. Through the door on the left is Northwell Health's Feinberg Division, which is available to service members, veterans, and their families but primarily provides outpatient care to veterans' family members; through the doors on the right is the VA Clinic at Bay Shore, which offers outpatient behavioral health and primary care services to veterans. The different sides of the center house separate receptions and display different signage, furniture, and decor. The IT infrastructure for both organizations is housed in a small room on the Feinberg Division side of the center. At the back of the facility, there are two locations designated for shared and common use, both of which are located on the Feinberg Division side of the facility: a conference room for clinicians from both sides to use when coordinating the care of veterans and their families and a kitchen (refrigerator, microwave, and storage space) to further encourage interaction among the UBHC team. A floor plan for the facility is provided in Figure 3.3.

Center Staffing

The Feinberg Division staff has an interdisciplinary team of clinicians. The staff currently includes three full-time clinical psychologists (one is also the director, who devotes half his time to clinical work and half to administration), a part-time psychology trainee, and a child and adolescent psychiatrist with a focus on trauma (see Table 3.2). The VA Clinic at Bay Shore's staff members represent multiple disciplines, includes a psychiatrist, a part-time psychologist, a nurse, social workers for general counseling and substance use counseling, and a psychiatrist for substance use counseling. The Feinberg Division and VA Clinic at Bay Shore sides employ separate receptionists who serve multiple roles—e.g., check-in, initial screening, scheduling, and managing patient charts. Because of increased clinic volume, after the first year of operation, the UBHC increased psychiatry and psychology trainee hours on the Feinberg Division side and expanded the social work staffing on the VA Clinic at Bay Shore side from part to full time. The VA Clinic at Bay Shore also recently added another part-time psychiatrist, both to meet patient demand and to provide a choice of a male or female provider at the site. In addition to staff on-site at the VA Clinic at Bay Shore, some providers located at the Northport VAMC participate in the collaboration (i.e., collaborate on the care of patients who have family members receiving care in the Feinberg Division) through video conferencing.

Figure 3.3
Physical Layout of Center

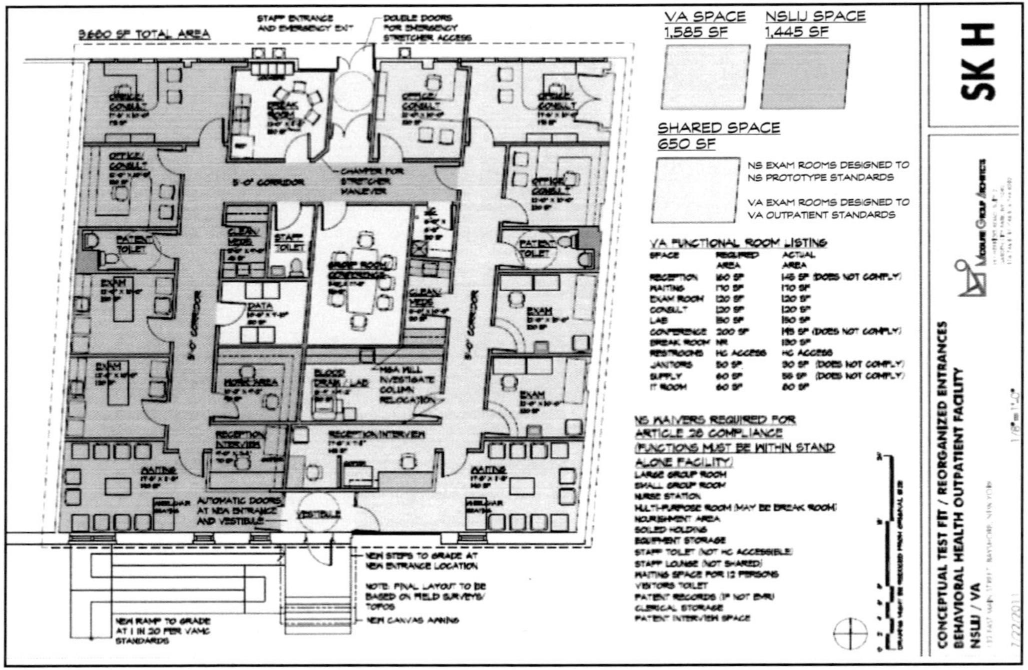

SOURCE: Provided by the UBHC.
NOTE: SF = square feet; NSLIF = North Shore LIJ (Northwell Health's previous name).
RAND *RR1647-3.3*

Table 3.2
Unified Behavioral Health Center Staffing for Behavioral Health

Title	VA Clinic at Bay Shore (number of full-time employees)	Feinberg Division (number of full-time employees)
Psychiatrist	0.6	0.4
Psychologist	0.2	2.5
Psychiatric registered nurse	0.6	0
Social worker	0.6	0
Addiction therapist	0.2	0
Addiction psychiatrist	0.2	0
Medical support assistant	0.5	0
Psychology trainee	0	0.4
Administration	<0.1	0.75
Administrative support	1.0	1.0

SOURCE: RWJF, 2015.

Northwell Health's leadership reported that they recognized that not all of their providers would have either interest in or experience with the UBHC's unique type of care for veterans and their family members. The leadership reported that they began the hiring process by selecting a psychologist who would serve as the director. Priority in hiring clinicians and staff at the UBHC was given to those who displayed a passion for the population to be treated, a collaborative approach to care, and expertise in trauma and evidence-based practices.

The VA staff assigned to the UBHC was initially made up of providers from the two CBOCs that the Northport VAMC had recently shuttered. There were no new hires for the VA Clinic at Bay Shore, and all VA providers split their time between the UBHC and at least one other location (e.g., the Northport VAMC or another CBOC). Those we spoke with indicated that the local VA leadership aimed to identify staff who would be the most suitable for the unique UBHC setting—

that is, individuals who were particularly flexible and collaborative in their work.

Northwell Health administrators reported difficulties in recruiting staff for the UBHC, most notably because of the location of the center in Suffolk County, approximately two hours by car from Manhattan. Administrators reported that although the location of the UBHC on Long Island was not necessarily ideal for attracting new behavioral health clinicians graduating from trainee programs, many of whom lived in Manhattan, administrators were committed to attracting staff who were a good fit for the center. For example, administrators have allocated resources, such as train fare, to support psychology fellows who intern at the center and who may eventually become employees. Northwell Health leadership reported that they also plan to apply for additional funding for hiring staff to meet the growing needs of the UBHC.

Staff Training

While UBHC staff reported that they received no specific training on collaborative or integrated care techniques for veterans and their families upon hiring, staff reported that they received on-the-job training on how best to deliver care in a collaborative model through numerous informal communications among staff, as well as weekly collaborative staff meetings. UBHC staff noted that at least once a month these meetings are devoted to training topics. For one team meeting, for instance, the local VA providers developed a short seminar that facilitated a discussion about the important and unique circumstances facing military families.

In addition, Feinberg Division leadership reported that they encourage and offer funding for their providers to attend conferences and continuing education courses that offer training in evidence-based practices (EBPs). There are no specific requirements or provisions for all staff to obtain training, supervision, and certification in a standard set of EBPs; however, specific staff members have received training and sometimes supervision and certification in specific EBPs. Each practitioner is pursuing certifications in the areas in which he or she specializes (e.g., trauma, child therapy), and then the providers cross-inform each other to the extent possible.

For instance, one Feinberg Division staff member who is focusing on trauma has completed training and supervision in Cognitive Processing Therapy (CPT) and Emotionally Focused Therapy (EFT) for couples and certification in Prolonged Exposure (PE). Another staff member, who is focusing on children, has completed specialized training and certification in Trauma-Focused Cognitive Behavioral Therapy (TFCBT) for children and Attachment, Regulation, and Competency (ARC) therapy. In sum, there is an emphasis on training staff in EBPs, but the training is not currently systematic in nature and instead focuses on developing different areas of expertise in different staff members. Feinberg Division leadership reported that the cross-training approach is efficient and cost-effective given the small size of the center and the fact that the staffing has been changing over time and includes rotating fellows who are there for a relatively short period.

While the VA Clinic at Bay Shore does not have specialized trainings specific to the UBHC, the standard VA practice is to promulgate EBP trainings among behavioral health staff. In 2006, the VA launched a national training initiative to help its clinicians learn PE and CPT (McGuire, Schnurr, and Smith, 2015). Indeed, VA providers reported that they are trained through the VA in various EBPs, including CPT and PE. At least one provider was also trained through the VA in family interventions for serious psychiatric disorders—including Behavioral Family Therapy and Family Focused Therapy. In addition, at least one provider independently pursued non-VA training and certification in Eye-Movement Desensitization and Reprocessing, Cognitive Behavioral Therapy (CBT), and Rational Emotive Behavior Therapy.

In addition to clinical training, Feinberg Division and Northwell Health staff playing a management role in the UBHC received four days of communications training provided by RWJF (North Shore-LIJ Health System, 2014) to promote the program and develop products and ideas. The training covered various topics, including developing presentations, talking to the media, and developing outreach materials. Staff used the training to hone interview skills and improve outreach and messaging to potential child and family patients.

Information Systems

The VA side of the UBHC uses electronic health records and maintains no paper charts on the premises; at the time of RAND's site visit, the Feinberg Division maintained paper charts and was moving toward the use of electronic health records, which were implemented in April 2016. The Feinberg Division side also maintains electronic databases of patients, services provided, and outcome measures administered. One database tracks demographics, diagnoses, and treatment information (including treatment history, problem source, and primary clinician). Another tracks the services provided to each patient, along with the date of service and clinician who provided the service. The outcome measures database tracks scores and dates administered on patient-reported outcomes for all patients and their family members and also includes the demographic and military background for each person. Since paper charts do not exist at the VA Clinic at Bay Shore, and since VA personnel are the only ones with access to the electronic health records, no patient information or treatment plan documents are shared with non-VA personnel. Each side of the clinic maintains its own independent treatment plan for joint patients, and communication about specific patients occurs in person or via the phone. UBHC staff have discussed implementing a shared treatment plan that would reside on the Feinberg Division side, but this is not currently in place.

Performance Monitoring

The Feinberg Division side of the UBHC collects data on patient symptoms and functioning, patient satisfaction, and provider productivity. Clinical measures are monitored by the provider to track patient progress in meeting treatment goals. The Feinberg Division clinic director also reviews patient satisfaction and progress. Furthermore, the clinic director reviews a subset of charts and provides informal feedback to providers on their notes, treatment plans, and any other aspects of charting. There is also a peer-review process for chart review as part of the greater Northwell Health psychology department, in which three charts are reviewed every nine months, and peers provide feedback before submitting the review to the director of psychology for quality-assurance purposes.

In addition to these performance-monitoring measures, Northwell Health reported on indicators and benchmarks through the RWJF annual reports by highlighting the volume of patient visits, collaborative care cases between the Feinberg Division and the VA Clinic at Bay Shore, referrals from the VA (see, for example, Table 3.3), and program outreach. Regarding outreach, the Feinberg Division team reported that it engaged in 115 events that reached at least 4,299 individuals, while the Northport VAMC highlighted the UBHC collaboration in at least 168 events that reached 5,416 individuals (North Shore-LIJ Health System, 2015).

Productivity and operational data are tracked using patient appointments per day and utilization—that is, the length of appointments and the number of appointments per clinician. In its Feinberg Division, Northwell Health started tracking patients per day, copayment collection rates, and aggregate diagnoses to identify opportunities to increase productivity following the introduction of a new billing system on January 25, 2016. In addition to tracking productivity, Northwell Health leadership reported that they review a range of measures on a monthly basis, including no-show and cancellation rates versus kept appointments, percentage of patients not seen within 90 days, percentage of new patients, overall patient satisfaction, and patient-reported likelihood to recommend this program to another person. For instance, for child and adolescent therapy, Northwell Health leadership review how many children are engaged in treatment and whether they are reaching their goals. These measures are indicators of how the staff and center are performing, which Northwell

Table 3.3
Feinberg Division Unique Patients by Referral Source

Source	Frequency (*N*)	Percentage
VA	140	63
Friend/relative	38	17
Other	42	19

SOURCE: RWJF, 2015.

Health leadership can use to evaluate whether the Feinberg Division is meeting its RWJF grant objectives.

According to those we spoke with, the VA does not employ any performance-monitoring systems or measures that are specific to the UBHC. The VA does, however, routinely employ performance-monitoring approaches for the clinic as it would for any other VA facility, with performance measures encompassing patient satisfaction, ease of access, quality, and efficiency (see Assistant Deputy Under Secretary for Health for Policy and Planning, 1995). The VA Clinic at Bay Shore is run as a standard VA CBOC, according to standard VA procedures and reporting requirements.

Key Takeaways

- After about five months of construction, the UBHC treated its first patient in late 2012; it is up and running and delivering behavioral health services to veterans and their families.
- The partnership between the Feinberg Division and the VA Clinic at Bay Shore sides of the UBHC allows for convenient access to behavioral health services for veterans and family members and facilitates exchange of information between the different sides of the center, which can improve the coordination of care.
- However, the center is not designed to be fully integrated; rather, it colocates and coordinates care. It has two separate sides, managed under two different authorities, sets of procedures, and reporting requirements. One side serves veterans, while the other side is available to veterans and service members but primarily serves family members. The sides have separate entrances, information systems, and performance-monitoring processes. This arrangement allows for privacy and separation of care between veterans and families who are served at the UBHC. Patients who desire exchange of information between the two sides can sign a release.

CHAPTER FOUR

Processes of Care: Services Delivered and Patient Characteristics

Our evaluation of the center's processes of care examined the types of services offered, the demographic and behavioral health characteristics of clinic patients, and the services that patients received.

Services Offered

The UBHC provides outpatient services only. On the Feinberg Division side, available services include medication management, individual and group psychotherapy, couples therapy, family therapy, and child therapy. The UBHC emphasizes evidence-based treatments in a number of ways: Providers attend clinical conferences on evidence-based therapies, learn about such therapies during monthly collaborative meetings, and hear presentations from relevant speakers on a monthly basis. While the UBHC does not officially offer peer-support approaches, various peer-to-peer programs (e.g., support groups) can utilize the UBHC conference space, and UBHC patients are welcome to attend these groups.

Feinberg Division staff reported that their patients are treated with a combination of manualized psychotherapy approaches—such as CPT, PE, ARC, EFT, and TFCBT—and more-general CBT and Interpersonal Therapy approaches, depending on the clinical presentation. Staff also provide a well-received support group for spouses of veterans with PTSD.

Feinberg Division patients complete a battery of clinically relevant measures assessing psychological symptoms and functioning (determined by the provider according to a baseline assessment) at three-month intervals. These measures are used to inform patient care and can be shared with the VA staff working on the VA Clinic at Bay Shore side of the center if patients sign a release.

The VA Clinic at Bay Shore side of the UBHC follows standard VA policies and procedures for providing care; there are no official VA guidelines for providing care in this type of collaborative setting. However, clinical practice guidelines jointly issued by the VA and DoD require that the VA provide access to behavioral health EBPs, including CPT and PE for PTSD (VA, undated). The VA has practice guidelines for the following behavioral health domains: assessment and management of patients at risk for suicide, bipolar disorder (adults), major depressive disorder, PTSD, and substance use disorders. These guidelines detail specific decisionmaking processes and algorithms, assessment protocols, first-line pharmacotherapy interventions, and EBPs for psychotherapy that should be used by clinicians who provide behavioral health care in VA and DoD settings.

The VA Clinic at Bay Shore employs the VA-required standard screenings (e.g., for suicide risk, depression, TBI, PTSD, alcohol abuse, military sexual trauma, weight, smoking) for patients, some at intake and some during visits. According to VA Clinic at Bay Shore staff we spoke with, the measurements are built in as clinical reminders, and these scores are discussed with the patient in terms of what it means for their care. Providers may conduct additional assessments that they individually determine to be clinically appropriate.

Case-management services are not officially provided at the UBHC. However, the social workers on the VA side and the psychologist on the Feinberg Division side both reported that they identify organizations and resources for client needs on an informal basis. When linkage to external referrals is needed, UBHC staff facilitate assistance from the VA if the patient is VA-eligible, or they use the Veterans Health Alliance Long Island listserv to connect individuals to services and resources (e.g., housing).

Getting into Care

Feinberg Division

When the UBHC first opened, care was available immediately. At the time of our site visit, there was a waiting list to see a Feinberg Division provider. This suggests that demand for these services increased following the opening of the UBHC.

To seek services on the Feinberg Division side, no referrals or health plan enrollments are required. Veterans need not be enrolled or eligible for VA health care services to seek care on the Feinberg Division side. At intake, all potential patients receive an initial screening by the receptionist to confirm their military connection and that they are seeking treatment for a service-related issue. Patients scheduled for a visit at the Feinberg Division side are asked to complete four to five pages of forms regarding demographics, military background, medical history, and psychological evaluation (e.g., symptoms of depression and PTSD, TBI screening, family or marital functioning). After patients complete the intake packet at their first appointments, they complete intake interviews conducted by a psychiatrist or psychologist. The Feinberg Division does not officially accept walk-ins, but if somebody happens to walk in, the staff makes an attempt to triage the patient.

VA Clinic at Bay Shore

There is currently a waiting list for psychosocial services at the VA Clinic at Bay Shore but no wait for psychiatry. If a veteran does not want to wait, he or she can receive psychosocial care from a provider at a different location—someone who is supervised by a behavioral health provider at Bay Shore who is linked with the collaboration. Veterans who already have family members receiving care at the Feinberg Division receive priority for care at the VA Clinic at Bay Shore.

To access services at the VA Clinic at Bay Shore, veterans must be enrolled in the VHA. Once enrolled, the VA uses a referral and consultation system to schedule patients with particular providers. All behavioral health intakes go through a behavioral health call center at the Northport VAMC to ensure that the veteran can receive care within one day if there are urgent needs or within 14 days if there are no urgent behavioral health needs. However, veterans may express preferences as to where they would like to receive care (regardless of where they live), and a veteran could choose to wait longer than 14 days if he or she wants to wait for a preferred clinic. Alternatively, behavioral health patients can present as walk-ins at the Northport VAMC. Although the Bay Shore VA CBOC does not officially have a walk-in clinic as the Northport VAMC does, it does accommodate veterans who walk in, in accordance with VA mandates.

The patient-intake process on the VA side of the UBHC is the standard VA intake procedure; no special intake is done for this particular, CBOC, and no special outcome measures are administered. The standard behavioral health intake involves assessment and triage by a psychiatric nurse, which involves vital signs and a questionnaire packet, including the VA-required standard screenings if they are due (they are completed at specific intervals, and electronic clinical reminders pop up as appropriate). If it is a first behavioral health visit, the patient receives a diagnostic intake interview with a psychiatrist, as well as a suicide risk assessment. If new behavioral health patients are not enrolled in primary care, they receive a referral to primary care.

Patient Characteristics

Feinberg Division

Based on their administrative data, a total of 351 adults and 45 children were seen at the Feinberg Division since its opening in December 2012, including patients and "collaterals"—nonpatient family members who participated in treatment for the benefit of the patient. Table 4.1 shows demographic and clinical characteristics of these individuals.

Of all the adults engaged with the clinic between December 2012 and December 2015, 210 were primary patients (46 veteran and 164 nonveteran), and 141 were adult collaterals participating in the care of patients (50 veteran and 91 nonveteran). Adults who utilized the clinic were predominately white (79 percent) and between the ages of 18 and 45 (58 percent), regardless of whether they were patients or collaterals, veterans or nonveterans. Nonveteran patients, the largest group served

Table 4.1
Patient and Collateral Characteristics: Feinberg Division

		Adult Patients (*N* = 210)		Adult Collaterals (*N* = 141)		
Characteristic	**All Adults (*N* = 351)**	**Veteran (*N* = 46)**	**Non-Veteran (*N* = 164)**	**Veteran (*N* = 50)**	**Non-Veteran (*N* = 91)[a]**	**Children (*N* = 45)**
Demographics						
Mean age (SD)	43.46 (15.42)	46.20 (16.00)	43.34 (15.46)	44.78 (15.87)	37.75 (12.50)	12.40 (3.71)
	%	%	%	%	%	%
Age distribution						
<18	–	–	–	–	–	88.89
18–45	58.27	54.35	56.71	57.50	75.00	11.11
45–65	28.42	28.26	31.71	20.00	21.43	0
65+	13.31	17.39	11.59	22.50	3.57	0
Male	41.60	84.78	14.63	94.00	39.56	51.11
Race/ethnicity						
White	79.35	78.26	77.44	80.49	92.00	62.79
African American	7.25	13.04	6.10	7.32	4.00	18.60
Hispanic	10.51	8.69	12.80	7.32	4.00	18.60
Asian/Pacific Islander/Alaska Native	2.17	0	3.66	0	0	0
Other	0.72	0	0	4.88	0	0
Education						
High school or less	25.00	37.77	23.78	21.62	13.64	100.00
Some college	34.33	42.22	29.88	40.54	40.91	0
College graduate or above	40.67	19.99	46.34	37.84	45.46	0
Employment						
Unemployed	24.54	41.30	19.75	34.21	8.70	2.33
Employed	57.25	41.30	62.96	39.47	78.26	0
Student	3.72	2.17	4.32	0	8.70	97.67
Retired	14.50	15.22	12.96	26.32	4.35	0

Table 4.1—Continued

Characteristic	All Adults (N = 351)	Adult Patients (N = 210)		Adult Collaterals (N = 141)		Children (N = 45)
		Veteran (N = 46)	Non-Veteran (N = 164)	Veteran (N = 50)	Non-Veteran (N = 91)[a]	
Family income						
Under $25,000	16.26	24.24	15.75	12.00	11.11	13.64
$25,000–$39,999	9.85	9.09	9.45	20.00	0	27.27
$40,000–$49,999	3.94	3.03	2.36	4.00	16.67	18.18
$50,000–$74,999	16.26	6.06	18.90	16.00	16.67	22.73
$75,000–$99,999	17.73	12.12	17.32	28.00	16.67	4.55
$100,000+	9.36	12.12	7.87	4.00	22.22	0
Did not endorse	26.60	33.33	28.35	16.00	16.67	13.64
Currently married	63.31	46.67	63.98	70.45	75.00	–
Former military characteristics						
Military/veteran affiliation						
Current active duty	4.84	–	7.32	–	5.49	0
Currently in reserve component	1.14	–	2.44	–	0	0
Veteran (former military)	27.35	100.00	–	100.00	–	0
Military/veteran child	8.26	–	13.41	–	7.69	95.56
Military/veteran spouse	28.77	–	59.15	–	4.40	0
Military/veteran other family	25.07	–	7.93	–	82.42	4.44
Close relationship with veteran	4.56	–	9.76	–	0	0

Table 4.1—Continued

		Adult Patients (*N* = 210)		Adult Collaterals (*N* = 141)		
Characteristic	All Adults (*N* = 351)	Veteran (*N* = 46)	Non-Veteran (*N* = 164)	Veteran (*N* = 50)	Non-Veteran (*N* = 91)[a]	Children (*N* = 45)
Branch of service affiliation						
Army	–	41.94	–	61.54	–	–
Navy	–	22.58	–	7.69	–	–
Marines	–	19.35	–	19.23	–	–
Air Force	–	6.45	–	7.69	–	–
National Guard	–	0	–	0	–	–
Army Reserve	–	6.45	–	0	–	–
Navy Reserve	–	3.23	–	3.85	–	–
Coast Guard	–	0	–	0	–	–
Conflict location (patients only)						
Operations Enduring Freedom, Iraqi Freedom, New Dawn	–	40.00		–	–	–
Persian Gulf	–	8.89	–	–	–	–
Vietnam	–	15.56	–	–	–	–
Other conflict[b]	–	17.78	–	–	–	–
Never deployed	–	17.78	–	–	–	–
Treatment history						
Never treated	42.75	26.09	50.00	20.00	58.82	58.54
Medication and psychotherapy	32.94	47.83	24.07	63.33	23.53	12.20
Medication management	6.27	10.87	5.56	3.33	5.88	7.32
Psychotherapy	18.04	15.22	20.37	13.33	11.76	21.95

Table 4.1—Continued

Characteristic	All Adults (N = 351)	Adult Patients (N = 210): Veteran (N = 46)	Adult Patients (N = 210): Non-Veteran (N = 164)	Adult Collaterals (N = 141): Veteran (N = 50)	Adult Collaterals (N = 141): Non-Veteran (N = 91)[a]	Children (N = 45)
Primary diagnosis (patients only)						
Depressive disorder	–	19.51	24.34	–	–	7.14
PTSD	–	36.59	1.97	–	–	4.76
Adjustment disorder	–	24.39	40.79	–	–	59.52
Anxiety disorder	–	2.44	15.13	–	–	11.90
Bipolar/mood disorder	–	4.88	3.29	–	–	4.76
Relational/ psychosocial disorder	–	2.44	11.18	–	–	7.14
Other	–	9.76	3.29	–	–	4.76

NOTE: SD = standard deviation.

[a] All 91 nonveteran collateral adults reported on gender and military affiliation. Between 17 and 28 reported on all other demographics. Because only ten nonveteran collaterals reported branch of service affiliation of self or family member, this information was omitted from the table.

[b] Includes deployments in Bosnia, Cuba, Germany, Honduras, Lebanon, and World War II and in peacetime (i.e., no conflict).

by the Feinberg Division, were predominately female (only 15 percent male), whereas veteran patients were predominately male (85 percent). Most nonveteran patients and collaterals were employed (63 percent and 78 percent, respectively), whereas only 41 percent of veteran patients and 39 percent of veteran collaterals were employed. Most adults endorsed having at least some college education (75 percent, combining the "some college" and "college graduate" categories from Table 4.1) and about half reported an average family income of under $75,000 (looking across income categories in Table 4.1), across all adult groups. The majority of all adults were currently married (63 percent).

Across all adults who utilized the center, 27 percent were veterans, 29 percent were military or veteran spouses, and 25 percent were other military or veteran family members (i.e., not spouses or children). In particular, nonveteran adult patients were predominately military or veteran spouses (59 percent), while nonveteran adult collaterals were predominately other family members (82 percent). Veteran patients had predominately served in the Army (42 percent), Navy (23 percent), and Marines (19 percent). A plurality (40 percent) of veteran patients reported serving in recent Operation Enduring Freedom, Operation Iraqi Freedom, and Operation New Dawn conflicts.

Among nonveteran adult patients, one-half (50 percent) reported no history of previous behavioral health treatment; nearly one-third (30 percent) reported history of treatment with psychiatric medication, either alone (24 percent) or in conjunction with psychotherapy (6 percent); and 20 percent reported treatment with psychotherapy alone. Among adult veteran patients, only 26 percent reported no history of previous behavioral health treatment; more than one-half (58 percent) reported history of treatment with psychiatric medication, either alone (48 percent) or in conjunction with psychotherapy (11 percent); and 15 percent reported treatment with psychotherapy alone.

Among nonveteran adult patients, adjustment disorders (41 percent) and depression (24 percent) were the most-common psychiatric diagnoses. In contrast, among veteran patients, PTSD was the most common diagnosis (37 percent), followed by adjustment disorders (24 percent) and depression (20 percent).

Among children seen at the clinic, 43 were patients and two were child collaterals (i.e., family members who participated in treatment for the benefit of the patient). All children seen at the Feinberg Division are included in Table 4.1, since child collaterals are such a small group. The majority of the children were white (63 percent), about one-half were male (51 percent), and their mean age was a little over 12 years old (SD = 3.71). The Feinberg Division's database tracked as children five young adult children (ages 18–20) of patients because they were younger than 18 on their admittance dates; therefore, we include them as children here. A majority (59 percent) of children's households had a family income of less than $50,000, unlike adult patients, who had higher incomes.

Among child patients, more than one-half (59 percent) reported no history of previous behavioral health treatment; 19 percent reported history of treatment with psychiatric medication, either alone (12 percent) or in conjunction with psychotherapy (7 percent); and 22 percent reported treatment with psychotherapy alone. Adjustment disorder (60 percent) was the most common psychiatric diagnosis, followed by anxiety (12 percent), depression (7 percent), and relational disorders (7 percent).

VA Clinic at Bay Shore

According to data provided by the VA, a total of 946 patients received behavioral health treatment at the VA Clinic at Bay Shore between November 2012 and January 2016. Table 4.2 shows characteristics of patients seen at this CBOC. The vast majority of veterans were male (93 percent) and white (82 percent). Approximately one-half (53 percent) of patients were over age 65. Most veterans had experienced combat, which may increase their vulnerability to behavioral health problems. Veterans' combat service spanned different eras: Operation Enduring Freedom, Operation Iraqi Freedom, and Operation New Dawn (20 percent); Persian Gulf (23 percent); or Vietnam (36 percent). Depression was the most frequently diagnosed psychiatric disorder among patients seen at the VA clinic (38 percent), followed by anxiety (34 percent) and PTSD (30 percent). Table 4.2 summarizes characteristics of all behavioral health patients utilizing the VA Clinic at Bay Shore, in comparison to all service users (i.e., adult patients and collaterals and children, veterans and nonveterans) of the Feinberg Division. The populations served are similar with respect to race and ethnicity, but VA Clinic at Bay Shore patients are predominately male and the majority of Feinberg Division patients are female, and the VA Clinic at Bay Shore serves more older adults (older than 65) than the Feinberg Division.

Service Utilization

Feinberg Division

The Feinberg Division side of the clinic provided behavioral health treatment to a total of 210 adult patients and 43 child patients over a three-year period, from December 2012 to December 2015.

Table 4.2
Patient Characteristics at the VA Clinic at Bay Shore (as Compared with All Users of the Feinberg Division)

Characteristics	VA Clinic at Bay Shore (N = 946)	Feinberg Division (N = 396)
Demographics		
Mean age (SD)	43.85 (15.47)	39.13 (17.95)
	%	%
Age distribution		
<18	–	12.38
18–45	22.10	51.70
45–65	35.48	24.46
65+	52.90	11.46
Male	93.36	42.68
Ethnicity		
Caucasian	81.64	77.12
African American	13.07	8.78
Hispanic	5.71	11.60
Other	0.41	2.50
Former military characteristics[a]		
Branch of service		
Army	54.70	55.56
Navy	17.74	9.94
Marines	14.53	18.71
Air Force	10.58	8.77
National Guard	–	2.92
Army Reserve	–	2.34
Navy Reserve	–	1.75
Coast Guard	0.96	–

Table 4.2—Continued

Characteristics	VA Clinic at Bay Shore (*N* = 946)	Feinberg Division (*N* = 396)
Conflict		
Operations Enduring Freedom, Iraqi Freedom, New Dawn	20.11	54.98
Persian Gulf	22.57	5.18
Vietnam	36.02	21.91
Other or never deployed	21.29	17.93
Prisoner of war status		
Yes	0.31	–
No	58.61	–
Unknown	43.78	–
Primary diagnosis		
Depressive disorder	37.80	20.34
PTSD	30.37	8.47
Adjustment disorder	21.07	41.10
Anxiety disorder	33.90	12.29
Bipolar disorder	9.00	3.81
Relational disorder	–	9.32
Schizophrenia	5.97	–
Other	–	4.66

[a] For the Feinberg Division, military variables may refer to either the individual or the individual's family member if the individual is not personally affiliated with the military.

Clinicians provided adult patients with 3,797 individual therapy sessions and a total of 325 diagnostic interviews, as well as 1,184 family therapy sessions, 749 group therapy sessions, and 50 group family therapy sessions, with an additional 11 visits for other types of psychological or psychiatric services (see Table 4.3). Most patients (93 percent) participated in a diagnostic interview or exam with a provider, and a majority (78 percent) also received individual therapy services. Approximately one-half of Feinberg Division patients received family therapy (48 percent) and attended appointments for psychiatric medication management or evaluation (45 percent), 15 percent received group therapy, and 2 percent received multifamily group therapy (i.e., group therapy composed of multiple families). Adult patients also received services from different kinds of behavioral health providers: 87 percent of patients received services from a (licensed) psychologist, and 68 percent received services from a psychiatrist. Nearly one-quarter (24 percent) of patients received services from a psychology fellow (trainee).

Although the Feinberg Division treated a relatively small number of patients, it provided a relatively large number of services per patient, on average. Table 4.4 shows the number of visits per patient at the Feinberg Division by type of behavioral health service. The average number of diagnostic visits per patient was between one and two sessions. Patients attended a median of 16.0 sessions of individual therapy. Individuals who participated in family therapy attended a median of 5.5 sessions, and those who participated in group therapy attended a median of 17.5 sessions. There was considerable variability in number of sessions across patients for all services types. For comparison, a previous RAND evaluation found that veterans receiving services from the VA reported, on average, about 12 mental health visits in a year, a lower number than Feinberg Division patients (Watkins et al., 2011), and findings from a national database found that patients receive, on average, fewer than five sessions of psychotherapy (Hansen, Lambert, and Forman, 2002).

Clinicians provided individual therapy to 79 percent of child patients, for a total of 900 sessions. The clinic also provided a total of 64 diagnostic interview sessions to 91 percent of child patients and 277 family therapy sessions to 72 percent of child patients (see Table 4.3). Child patients received services from different kinds of behavioral health providers: 91 percent of patients received services from a (licensed) psychologist, and 63 percent received services from a

Table 4.3
Behavioral Health Service Encounters by Service Type Across Clinics

	Feinberg Division					
	Adult Patients (*N* = 210)		Child Patients (*N* = 43)		VA Clinic at Bay Shore (*N* = 936)	
Service	**Encounters (*N*)**	**Patients Using Service (%)**	**Encounters (*N*)**	**Patients Using Service (%)**	**Encounters (*N*)**	**Adult Patients Using Service (%)**
Diagnostic exam/ interview	325	92.86	64	90.7	3,528	70.30
Individual therapy	3,797	77.62	900	79.07	3,061	66.77
Family therapy	1,184	47.62	277	72.09	–	–
Multifamily group therapy	50	2.38	–	–	–	–
Group therapy	749	15.24	1	2.33	301	2.14
Follow-up visit for evaluation/ management of established patient	786	44.76	77	34.88	–	–
Individual substance use therapy	–	–	–	–	310	8.23
Group substance use therapy	–	–	–	–	634	3.21
Other behavioral health service	11	4.29	3	4.65	–	–

Table 4.4
Service Utilization by Patients at the Feinberg Division

	Adults (*N* = 210)			Children (*N* = 43)		
Service	Median Number of Sessions per Patient	Mean Number of Sessions per Patient (SD)	Range of Number of Sessions per Patient	Median Number of Sessions per Patient	Mean Number of Sessions per Patient (SD)	Range of Number of Sessions per Patient
Diagnostic exam/ interview	2.0	1.67 (0.75)	1–2	2.0	1.64 (0.63)	1–2
Individual therapy	16.0	23.29 (23.24)	4–36	19.5	26.47 (21.07)	13–36
Family therapy	5.5	11.84 (13.69)	2–18	5.0	8.94 (8.79)	2–14
Group therapy	17.5	23.41 (25.72)	2–28	1.0	1.00 (–)	1–1
Multifamily group therapy	11.0	10.00 (2.00)	9–11	–	–	–
Follow-up visit for evaluation/ management of established patient	6.0	8.36 (7.37)	2–12	3.0	5.13 (4.52)	2–10
Other behavioral health service	1.0	1.22 (0.67)	1–1	1.5	1.50 (0.71)	1–2

psychiatrist. More than a quarter (28 percent) of patients received services from a psychology fellow (trainee).

Table 4.4 illustrates that child patients attended a median of 19.5 sessions of individual therapy. Children who participated in family therapy attended a median of 5.0 sessions. There was considerable variability in number of sessions across patients for all services administered to child patients.

VA Clinic at Bay Shore

Between November 2012 and January 2016, the VA reported that 936 unique patients were seen in the CBOC, for a total of 7,802 behavioral health visits. Across all these patients, individuals attended a median of five behavioral health clinic sessions (mean = 7.88; SD = 10.88), but there was a significant variation in number of sessions per patient (range = 1–102 sessions).

The VA Clinic at Bay Shore provided a number of different services to a large volume of patients, as compared with the Feinberg Division (see Table 4.3). Most of the CBOC patients (70 percent) attended one or more psychiatric diagnostic appointments in the clinic, for a total of 3,528 patient encounters. A majority (84 percent) of CBOC patients attended individual therapy sessions, and a small minority (2 percent) received group behavioral health treatment. Additionally, 3 percent of patients received individual therapy for a substance use disorder, and 8 percent received group therapy for a substance use disorder. Most patients in the behavioral health clinic were seen by a psychiatrist (79 percent) for individual psychotherapy or medication management appointments. Approximately 15 percent of patients were seen by a psychologist or clinical social worker, and 3 percent received treatment for a substance use disorder from an addiction counselor. Table 4.5 shows the number of visits per patient for different types of behavioral health services. Individuals attended a median of six individual therapy sessions and a median of eight group therapy sessions. Among individuals who received substance use counseling, patients attended a median of one individual session and 12 group counseling sessions. Individuals varied with respect to the number of sessions they attended for each type of service (Table 4.5).

Key Takeaways

- The UBHC provided behavioral health care to a significant number of patients over the course of three years, which was noteworthy considering that it was a new center ramping up its capac-

Table 4.5
Service Utilization by Patients at the VA Clinic at Bay Shore

Service	Median Number of Sessions per Patient (*N* = 936 patients)	Mean number of Sessions per Patient (*N* = 936 patients)	Range (*N* = 936 patients)
Individual therapy	6	7.22 (8.86)	1–101
Group therapy	8	13.74 (15.00)	1–57
Individual substance use therapy	1	3.76 (6.02)	1–33
Group substance use therapy	12	20.15 (23.42)	1–102

ity to provide care (e.g., through staffing) and reaching out to potential patients in the community for the first time.

- The VA Clinic at Bay Shore saw many more patients than did the Feinberg Division side. This is partly expected because the VA Clinic at Bay Shore is able to receive direct referrals from within the VA health system, whereas the Feinberg Division relies on its own outreach, advertising, and word of mouth to attract new patients. While the Feinberg Division treated many fewer patients, it provided more-intensive treatment; for instance, VA Clinic at Bay Shore patients received a median of six individual therapy sessions, whereas Feinberg Division patients received a median of 16 individual therapy sessions. As a result, the overall number of encounters of patient care was comparable across the two sides of the UBHC despite the very different patient loads.
- While the two sides of the center had different patterns of service utilization (VA Clinic at Bay Shore provided fewer services to a larger number of individuals, while the Feinberg Division provided more services to a smaller number of individuals), both sides succeeded in getting up and running and delivering a lot of services in a relatively short time frame (three years).

CHAPTER FIVE

Patient Experiences and Outcomes

To assess the effects of care on patients treated at the UBHC, we used interviews to collect data on patient experiences with care and analyzed data on patient-reported outcome measures collected by Northwell Health clinic staff.

Patient Experiences

Overall, UBHC patients we interviewed reported having good access to care. Patients reported that they appreciated the fact that the UBHC accommodated them by scheduling multiple visits in one day to reduce the number of trips. Patients reported few barriers to care, noting reasonable wait times and an easy and user-friendly scheduling experience. Patients appreciated that there were no co-payments for their care, making their care at the UBHC affordable.

The majority of UBHC patients we spoke with noted that the location of the facility was convenient for them. For patients who described the distance to the facility as a "hassle," they noted that the benefits of the services they receive outweighed the inconvenience and cost of getting to the site.

Patients reported being extremely satisfied with the care they received. On a clinic administered patient satisfaction survey, 110 patient respondents (86 percent) who received care on the Feinberg Division side of the UBHC agreed or strongly agreed with the statement, "I like the services I received here." Further, 108 patients (89 percent) agreed or strongly agreed that they "would recommend this agency to a friend or family member."

During site visit interviews, patients pointed to the UBHC as filling a special niche in their community and offered numerous reasons why they would prefer to seek care at the UBHC rather than from other behavioral health providers. One of the key reasons cited was a sense that other community providers do not understand PTSD and its impact on families. As one patient put it, "We are usually teaching other providers about PTSD and not discussing our issues." The patients with whom we spoke also indicated the importance of a place where veterans' families can get care that is attuned to the needs of veterans. Indeed, some veterans with PTSD with whom we spoke described feeling "demonized" when they sought care at other settings because the therapists there did not understand how PTSD affected their behavior. Patients we interviewed reported valuing the UBHC staff's knowledge of PTSD and the center's affiliation with the VA. Several veterans' spouses reported a feeling that they had no place to go before the UBHC opened. According to one spouse we spoke with, the UBHC "is a place for families to go that is familiar with veterans' issues." Patients also reported a sense of camaraderie with the other veterans and veterans' families at the UBHC, noting that it feels like a community.

In our interviews, patients expressed appreciation that staff at the UBHC work collaboratively with each other, both within and across the two sides of the clinic. Many veterans reported receiving individual therapy services on the VA Clinic at Bay Shore side of the UBHC; while some go to the Feinberg Division side for individual therapy, others have kept their individual therapy at the Northport VAMC because they had long-standing relationships there. And at least one veteran we spoke with reported that he did not want his individual therapist to provide services to his family; he preferred to keep his family and individual therapist separate. However, most patients interviewed did not share that sentiment. Many veteran family members reported that they found it convenient that they could receive services in the same place as their spouses or partners, and many found it advantageous to receive individual and couples therapy that is coordinated, thus making their care "more cohesive." The patients we spoke with also appeared to recognize the benefits of having information shared between providers who are treating different members of a family. One patient noted that "when [providers] communicate, it's fantastic," and another observed that "they are all on the same page with each other." Some patients also realized that the collaborative nature of their care meant that they did not have to repeat themselves—for example, they did not have to spend a couples therapy session catching up on what was discussed in an individual session—and were thus able to make better use of their therapy time.

Patients characterized the care they have received at the UBHC as high quality. All focus group participants reported that they were satisfied with their care, and some went so far as to suggest that the care they received at the UBHC had saved their marriages, or even their lives. Patients reported not only benefiting personally from the UBHC services but also becoming better caregivers to their families after receiving care. Reports about the UBHC staff have been very enthusiastic (e.g., "I really love the people here," "I've never met such a wonderful group of people"), and patients perceive the staff to be caring and accommodating.

Adult Outcome Measures

The current evaluation relied on previously collected outcome data, which were only available for patients treated on the Feinberg Division side of the UBHC. The Feinberg Division side of the center routinely collects patient-reported outcome data on individuals treated in the clinic at three-month intervals (the median duration of treatment was about nine months, including patients who were still in treatment when we received the data and who may ultimately have a longer treatment duration than calculated). All patients completed the clinically relevant (determined by the provider according to the baseline assessment) follow-up assessments at three-month intervals. For instance, if a patient presented with depressive symptoms, the clinic monitored those symptoms every three months; however, not everyone whose depressive symptoms were monitored had a depression diagnosis. Similarly, only those who had PTSD symptoms routinely completed relevant outcomes measures, and only those who completed couples or family treatment received couples or family measures. We utilized all available outcome data in the evaluation, including data collected on collaterals who were not the primary patients being treated. We also included data on a small number of older child patients who were administered adult outcome measures in addition to child measures (e.g., six adolescent patients completed the BDI-II in addition to the YSR).

To examine the extent to which treatment dropout might contribute to bias in the results, we compared baseline depressive and anxiety symptoms between individuals who only completed one assessment with those who went on to complete follow-up assessments. Two-sample *t*-tests revealed no differences in either baseline depressive symptoms ($t = -0.30$, *ns*) or baseline anxiety symptoms ($t = 0.86$, *ns*) between those who did and did not complete follow-up assessments. Thus, those who completed follow-up assessments seem to be similar to those who did not. However, we do not know how results might change if further assessments were available for those who did not complete follow-ups, which is a limitation of the evaluation.

Depressive Symptoms Decreased

As measured by patient ratings on the BDI-II scale, depressive symptoms decreased significantly over the course of treatment. Adjusting for individual demographic characteristics (age, gender, ethnicity, education, income, and military status), BDI-II scores significantly declined over time following initial baseline assessment (see Table 5.1 and Figure 5.1). There was a significant mean treatment effect on depressive symptoms, such that patient scores declined by an average of 1.4 points (standard error [SE] = 0.23, $p < 0.001$) at each three-month assessment over the course of treatment. BDI-II scores were significantly lower at each subsequent point over treatment, compared with baseline scores (see Table 5.1), with patients achieving scores 5.8 points lower (SE = 1.06, $p < 0.001$) than baseline after one year of treatment.

To assess the extent to which the change over time was statistically significant and clinically meaningful, we examined the proportion of

Table 5.1
Change in Adult Outcomes over Time

	Depression (BDI-II)	Anxiety (BAI)	Family Functioning (FAD)[a]	Relationship Adjustment (DAS)[a]	Quality of Life (Q-LES-Q-SF)	PTSD (PCL-5)
Baseline score[b]	27.65 (5.62)	18.53 (5.52)	2.82 (0.53)	66.23 (23.55)	35.74 (5.61)	32.25 (14.44)
Mean treatment effect, overall	−1.40*** (0.23) N = 219	−0.63** (0.24) N = 215	−0.09** (0.03) N = 71[a]	3.48** (1.11) N = 68[a]	0.83** (0.25) N = 176	0.43 (1.01) N = 111
After 3 months in treatment	−2.29** (0.76) N = 135	−0.11 (0.77) N = 129	−0.03 (0.07) N = 26	3.42 (3.01) N = 27	1.56† (0.82) N = 99	−2.92 (2.75) N = 39
After 6 months in treatment	−3.66*** (0.85) N = 91	−1.45† (0.88) N = 83	−0.12 (0.10) N = 15	7.15* (3.45) N = 18	2.03* (0.93) N = 69	−1.74 (3.27) N = 23
After 9 months in treatment	−3.78*** (0.96) N = 67	−1.75† (0.97) N = 63	−0.30** (0.10) N = 15	12.93** (3.81) N = 14	2.37* (1.01) N = 60	0.65 (3.67) N = 17
After 1 year in treatment	−5.80*** (1.06) N = 52	−2.41* (1.10) N = 47	−0.28† (0.16) N = 6	7.01 (7.00) N = 4	3.55** (1.11) N = 46	4.80 (5.24) N = 7
Observations	526	497	168	163	391	162

[a] For FAD and DAS, *N* is the number of families, because individuals are nested in couples and families. For all other measures, *N* is the number of individuals.

[b] Baseline scores are intercepts in the corresponding mixed models with random slope.

† = $p < 0.10$; * = $p < 0.05$; ** = $p < 0.01$; *** = $p < 0.001$.

the sample that achieved a change of one-half of a standard deviation over six months. A half standard deviation was chosen because previous studies have shown that a change of this magnitude is highly likely to be clinically meaningful (e.g., Norman, Sloan, and Wyrwich, 2003; Schultz, Glickman, and Eisen, 2014); a six-month period was chosen to allow adequate time for change (e.g., Stulz and Lutz, 2007; Uher et al., 2011) and minimize attrition during the observation period (i.e., to maximize sample size, which decreases over time). A study of a nationally representative random sample of Operation Enduring Free-

Figure 5.1
Change in Depression Symptoms over Time

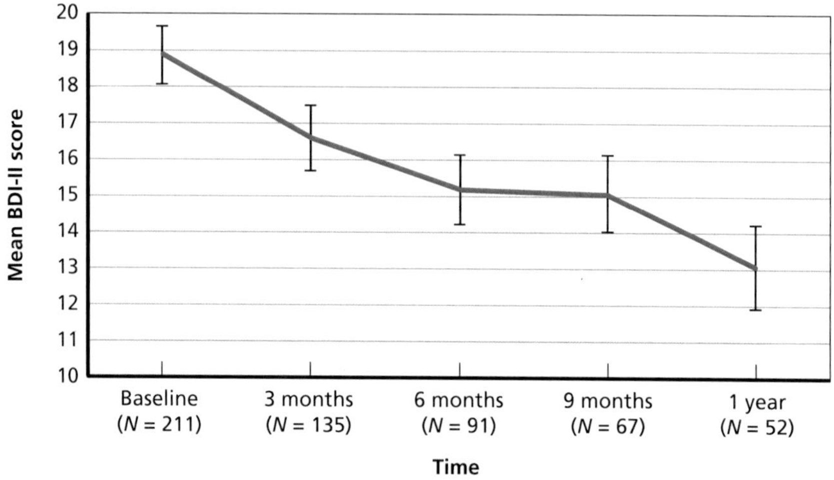

NOTE: Plotted values are model-based least-square means at each time point from a repeated measures mixed-effects model, controlled for age, gender, ethnicity, education, family income level, and military status. Error bars are standard errors.
RAND *RR1647-5.1*

dom and Operation Iraqi Freedom veterans surveyed within a year of returning from deployments found that only 26 percent showed a clinically meaningful improvement in mental health of half of a standard deviation over a six-month period, and only 23 percent showed a half standard deviation improvement in PTSD over six months (Schultz, Glickman, and Eisen, 2014).

In the current evaluation, we found that 65 percent of individuals achieved a clinically meaningful reduction of depressive symptoms of at least half a standard deviation lower than baseline.

Anxiety Symptoms Decreased

Adjusting for the same set of covariates, ratings of anxiety symptoms on the BAI scale decreased over the course of treatment (see Table 5.1 and Figure 5.2). There was a significant mean treatment effect across individuals, such that BAI scores declined by 0.63 points (SE = 0.24, $p < 0.001$) at each subsequent assessment over the course of treatment.

Figure 5.2
Change in Anxiety Symptoms over Time

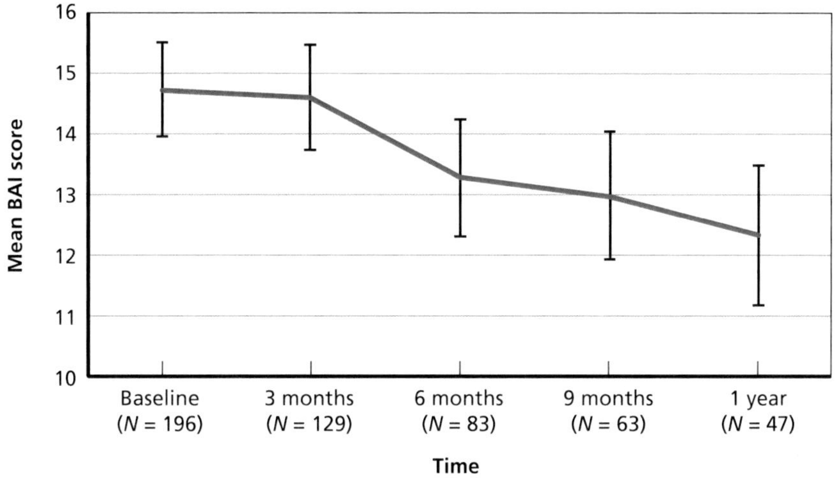

NOTE: Plotted values are model-based least-square means at each time point from a repeated measures mixed-effects model, controlled for age, gender, ethnicity, education, family income level, and military status. Error bars are standard errors.
RAND *RR1647-5.2*

There were trends ($p < 0.10$) toward lower scores at the six-month and nine-month assessments, compared with baseline, and scores at the 12-month assessment were significantly lower than baseline ratings. We ran an additional model to understand the impact of anxiety diagnosis on treatment effects and found that there was a significant interaction on BAI scores between current anxiety diagnosis and time, such that individuals with a current anxiety diagnosis demonstrated significant reductions in BAI scores at all subsequent assessments during treatment. At three months, scores among individuals with an anxiety diagnosis decreased by an additional 8.01 points (SE = 1.95, $p < 0.001$); at six months, by 9.54 points (SE = 2.33, $p < 0.001$); at nine months, by 6.95 points (SE = 2.69, $p < 0.01$); and at 12 months, by an additional 9.76 points (SE = 2.75, $p < 0.001$) relative to baseline. We found that 49 percent of patients achieved a clinically meaningful reduction of anxiety symptoms of at least half a standard deviation lower than their baseline scores over six months.

Family Functioning Improved

Patient ratings of problems with family functioning on the FAD also showed improvement over the course of treatment. Across individuals in treatment, there was a mean 0.09-point (SE = 0.03, $p < 0.001$) reduction—meaning that problems decreased—at each assessment over the course of treatment (see Table 5.1 and Figure 5.3). Ratings did not differ across all assessment points relative to baseline, but scores at the nine-month assessment were significantly lower (–0.30 points, SE = 0.10, $p < 0.001$). We found that 39 percent of patients achieved a clinically meaningful change in family functioning of at least half a standard deviation over six months.

Figure 5.3
Reduction in Problems with Family Functioning over Time

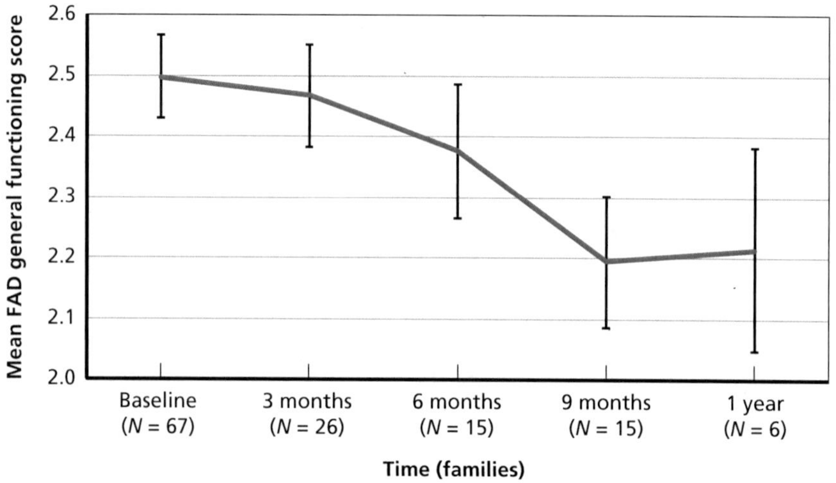

NOTE: Plotted values are model-based least-square means at each time point from a repeated-measures mixed-effects model, controlled for age, gender, ethnicity, education, family income level, and military status. Error bars are standard errors.
RAND *RR1647-5.3*

Relationships Improved

Patient ratings on the DAS of couples' relationship functioning increased significantly over the course of treatment (see Table 5.1 and Figure 5.4). There was a significant mean treatment effect, such that

Figure 5.4
Change in Relationship Functioning over Time

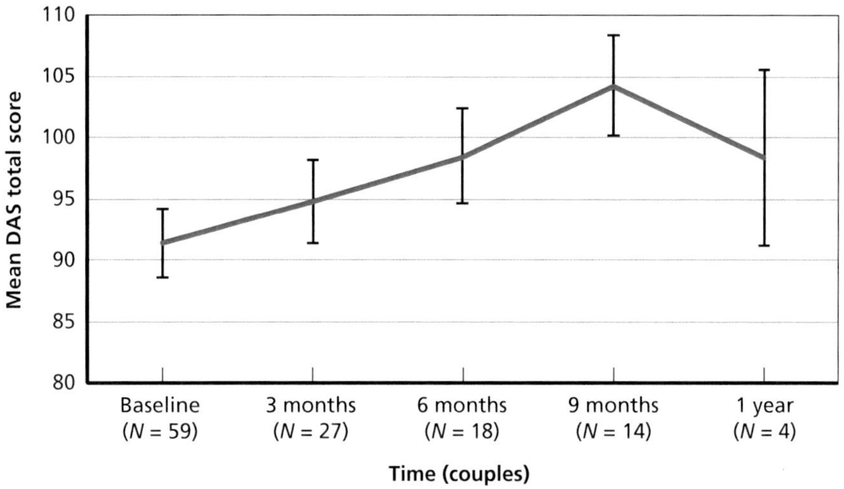

NOTE: Plotted values are model-based least-square means at each time point from a repeated-measures mixed-effects model, controlled for age, gender, ethnicity, education, family income level, and military status. Error bars are standard errors.
RAND *RR1647-5.4*

ratings improved by an average of 3.47 points (SE = 1.11, $p < 0.001$) at each three-month assessment. Ratings did not differ from baseline across all points, but there was a significant difference between DAS ratings at baseline and at the nine-month assessment (12.93 points, SE = 3.81, $p < 0.05$). We found that 47 percent of couples achieved a clinically meaningful change in relationship functioning of at least half a standard deviation over a six-month period.

Quality of Life and Satisfaction Increased

Ratings of quality of life enjoyment and satisfaction on the Q-LES-Q–SF also improved over the course of treatment (see Table 5.1 and Figure 5.5). There was a mean effect of treatment, such that scores increased by 0.83 points (SE = 0.25, $p < 0.001$) at each assessment. Relative to baseline, ratings were significantly higher at later assessment points (e.g., an increase of 3.55 points [SE = 1.11, $p < 0.001$] at the 12-month assessment) (see Table 5.1). We found that 52 percent of

Figure 5.5
Change in Quality-of-Life Enjoyment and Satisfaction over Time

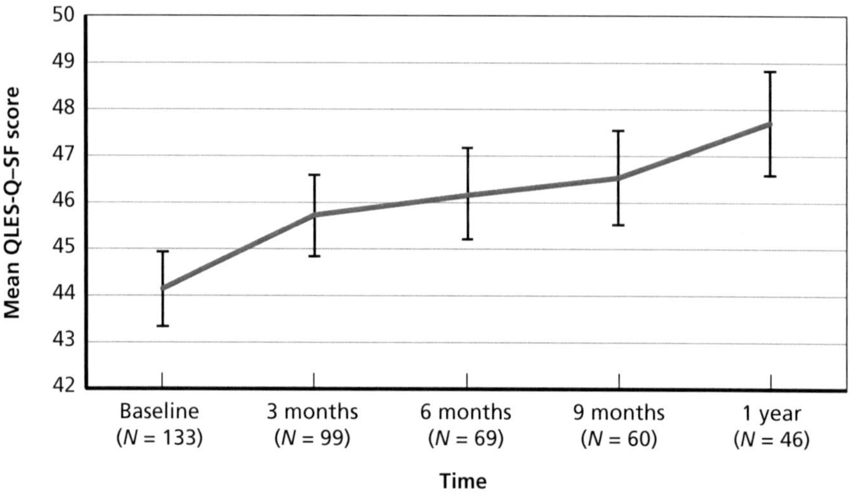

NOTE: Plotted values are model-based least-square means at each time point from a repeated-measures mixed-effects model, controlled for age, gender, ethnicity, education, family income level, and military status. Error bars are standard errors.
RAND *RR1647-5.5*

patients achieved a clinically meaningful improvement in quality of life of at least half a standard deviation from baseline over six months.

Half of Patients Experienced Clinically Significant Reductions in PTSD Symptoms

Ratings of PTSD symptoms on the PCL-5 did not change over the course of treatment compared with baseline (see Table 5.1 and Figure 5.6). Although changes in PCL were not statistically significant for the full sample, we found evidence of clinically significant change: 50 percent of patients achieved a clinically meaningful reduction of PTSD symptoms of at least half a standard deviation lower than baseline scores over six months (as compared with 23 percent in a nationally representative random sample of Operation Enduring Freedom and Operation Iraqi Freedom veterans; see Schultz, Glickman, and Eisen, 2014).

Figure 5.6
Posttraumatic Stress Symptoms over Time

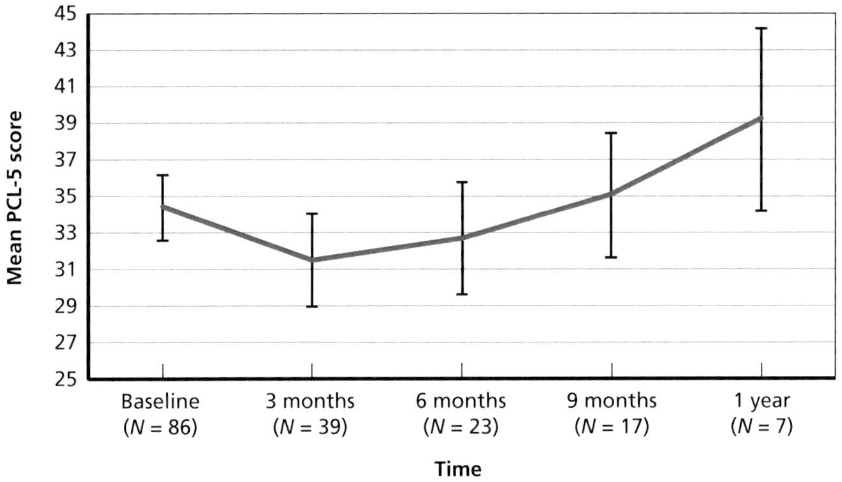

NOTE: Plotted values are model-based least-square means at each time point from a repeated-measures mixed-effects model, controlled for age, gender, ethnicity, education, family income level, and military status. Error bars are standard errors.
RAND *RR1647-5.6*

Child Outcome Measures

Children were only treated on the Feinberg Division side of the UBHC, so the outcome data below pertain to only that side of the center. As with adults, outcome data were collected about children at three-month intervals (the median duration of treatment was approximately eight months for children, including individuals who were still in treatment when we received the data). All patients completed measures from the Achenbach System of Empirically Based Assessments; parents of 42 children completed the parent-report measure (CBCL), and children who were 12 years and older ($N = 20$) completed the self-report version (YSR). For 18 children, both parent-report and self-report measures were completed.

Child Behavioral Health Symptoms Decreased

Controlling for respondent gender, parent ratings of child behavioral health symptoms on the CBCL showed overall reductions in child behavioral symptoms over the course of treatment, with mean decreases of 1.52 points (SE = 0.57, $p < 0.001$) at each three-month follow-up assessment. Compared with the baseline assessment, scores were significantly lower at the three-month and six-month assessments (see Table 5.2 and Figure 5.7). We found that 71 percent of patients achieved a clinically

Table 5.2
Change in Child Outcomes over Time

	Outcome	
	Parent Reports of Child Behavioral Health (CBCL)[a]	Youth Reports of Behavioral Health Problems (YSR)[b]
Baseline score[c] (SD)	60.60 (1.60)	36.88 (10.77)
Mean treatment effect, overall (SD)	−1.52** (0.57) *N* = 41[a]	−2.60*** (0.59) *N* = 20[b]
After 3 months in treatment	−4.29** (1.65) *N* = 18	−2.53 (1.73) *N* = 11
After 6 months in treatment	−5.53** (1.77) *N* = 14	−7.43*** (1.81) *N* = 10
After 9 months in treatment	−3.26 (2.09) *N* = 10	−8.12*** (2.28) *N* = 5
After 1 year in treatment	−5.65† (3.08) *N* = 4	−8.35** (2.80) *N* = 3
Total observations	100	47

[a] For CBCL, *N* is the number of families (i.e., the number of children reported on rather than the number of parent reports, as individuals are nested in families).

[b] For YSR, *N* is the number of children.

[c] Baseline scores are intercepts in the corresponding mixed models with random slope.

† = $p < 0.10$; * = $p < 0.05$; ** = $p < 0.01$; *** = $p < 0.001$.

Figure 5.7
Change in Parent Reports of Child Behavioral Health Problems over Time

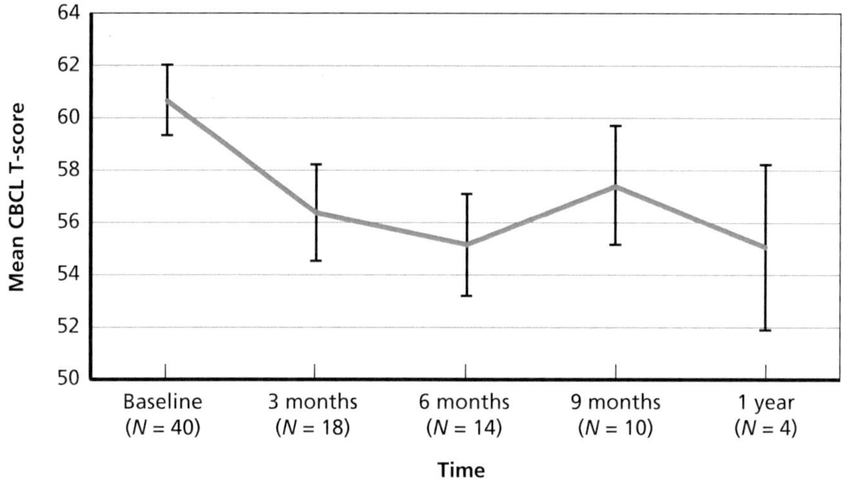

NOTE: Plotted values are model-based least-square means at each time point from a repeated measures mixed effects model, controlled for gender. Error bars are standard errors.

RAND *RR1647-5.7*

meaningful reduction in symptoms of at least half a standard deviation lower than their baseline scores over a six-month period.

Child Reports of Behavioral and Emotional Symptoms Also Showed Improvement

Similarly, after controlling for age, gender, and ethnicity, child self-reports of emotional and behavioral symptoms on the YSR showed decreases in symptoms over the course of treatment. There was a mean treatment effect, such that scores decreased by 2.6 points (SE = 0.59, $p < 0.001$) on average at each assessment. Scores were significantly lower compared with baseline at the six-month, nine-month, and 12-month assessments (see Table 5.2 and Figure 5.8). We found that 63 percent of patients achieved a clinically meaningful reduction in symptoms of at least half a standard deviation lower than baseline over a six-month period.

Figure 5.8
Change in Child Reports of Behavioral Health Symptoms over Time

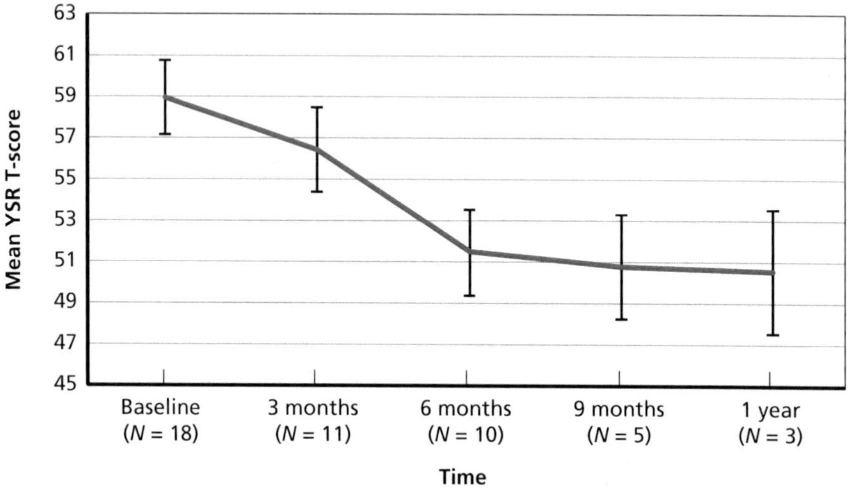

NOTE: Plotted values are model-based least-square means at each time point from a repeated-measures mixed-effects model, controlled for age, gender, and ethnicity. Error bars are standard errors.

RAND *RR1647-5.8*

Key Takeaways

- Adult patients treated on the Feinberg Division side of the UBHC showed improvement in key outcomes: symptoms of depression and PTSD, family functioning, and quality of life. Child patients showed improvements, with fewer behavioral problems.
- The UBHC patients we interviewed consistently expressed satisfaction with their experiences at the center and the care they received. In particular, focus group participants cited the benefits of colocated, coordinated, and cohesive care that is attuned to the needs of veteran families.

CHAPTER SIX

Lessons Learned, Recommendations, and Conclusions

In this final chapter, we outline lessons learned with respect to program implementation and implications for improving or replicating the UBHC model.

Issues for Sustaining and Replicating the Model

Implementation Barriers and Challenges

The funding model used in the first three years of implementation is likely not sustainable. The Feinberg Division provided its services at no charge for the first three years the center was open, so no revenue was generated for services administered. This may not be a sustainable funding model in the long run, as it relies on donations, philanthropic support, or other financial resources to pay for operating expenses. Recognizing this, Northwell Health has been working toward developing more-sustainable funding for the Feinberg Division throughout the life of the UBHC. As a result, Northwell Health implemented a billing system in the Feinberg Division as of January 25, 2016, in which insurance is billed and patients are charged a co-payment. Patients without insurance are charged on a sliding scale, depending on income. Feinberg Division leadership reported that most patients have not had a problem with the new billing system, but for some patients it is presenting a financial hardship. At the time of this writing, Northwell Health was still in the process of developing policies to assist those for whom care is a financial burden. Thus, Northwell Health has given clients with billing issues a grace period until the end of July 2016 while policies are being finalized. The potential impact of the new billing system on care utilization and patient satisfaction is not yet known. To avoid this implementation barrier, programs seeking to replicate the UBHC model might benefit from designing a sustainable funding plan prior to initiation of the program.

Northwell Health is a private entity and has been able to raise funds to support the UBHC costs. The VA side of the clinic is funded through the congressionally approved budget resources for the VHA that is allocated to VISN 3. The VA budget covers salaries for the staff, equipment, and IT for its side of the clinic but does not provide any other funds to support the UBHC.

Obtaining buy-in from local VA leadership proved challenging. Leadership of the Northport VAMC reported that the first challenge the UBHC faced was obtaining buy-in from some of the senior leaders at the Northport VAMC. While there were champions at the Northport VAMC promoting this collaboration, there were also skeptics. Some worried that the UBHC would potentially divert patients from the VA and from the local university with which it is affiliated. In addition, an earlier attempt to form a collaboration between Northwell Health and the Northport VAMC had failed. Northport VAMC leadership reported that the fact that Northwell Health provided all the funding for the center helped to assuage these concerns. The VA Central Office and Office of General Council expressed concerns throughout the planning process, but they saw the advantages of the program for veterans and conceptually agreed with it. Since this was a "groundbreaking" program, they were challenged in figuring out a way to make it work but did not stop the implementation process.

Coordinating the construction of a new facility that met the needs and regulations of both organizations was challenging. As noted, the RWJF grant and matching funds did not cover the cost of opening a new UBHC facility, an endeavor that was both expensive and logistically complicated. After a contractor deferred work on the location, the UBHC had to obtain design approvals from clinical and administrative leadership at both Northwell Health and the Northport

VAMC. The design then had to be reviewed by VA engineers to ensure that it met strict federal requirements. VA requirements for the facility were extensive, such as needing a separate locked location for computing hardware and a separate security system for the building. Then a lease had to be negotiated and agreed on by the VA legal team and the Northwell Health legal team. Once the lease was negotiated, construction finally began. Construction took a few months, and along the way, the team encountered many questions about the design of the center that had to be agreed on by both participating organizations. This was complicated by the fact that not all of the key individuals were involved from the start of the project. Northwell Health staff in charge of the construction project reported that while both clinical and facility staff were involved from Northwell Health, only facility staff were directly involved on the VA side. It also seemed to Northwell Health staff that not all of the key VA facility staff were initially involved, because different VA staff became involved shortly before the building opened, and the newly involved VA staff expressed several new concerns related to VA regulations for security and accessibility.

Absence of institutionalized and codified procedures may present challenges. VA Clinic at Bay Shore and Feinberg Division staff alike reported being challenged by the lack of designated-provider appointment slots for shared cases at the VA Clinic at Bay Shore and the lack of VA staff dedicated to collaborative care. However, designated slots and staff might not be a viable solution because of the VA's need to ensure timely access to care for all veterans, as discussed in the recommendations section below. VA Clinic at Bay Shore staff noted that there is currently no directive in the VA to implement these kinds of programs and services, and these staff expressed a desire for clear directives that would support collaboration and ensure that current effective strategies (e.g., a VA CBOC staff taking on a liaison role, prioritization of veterans who have family members receiving care in the Feinberg Division) are preserved in the event of staffing changes.

There were some logistical barriers to collaboration. Providers on both sides of the UBHC cited not being able to send secure emails containing patient information as a challenge that made collaboration more difficult. They reported that close communication was still possible by phone, in person, and through the VA Clinic at Bay Shore liaison, but it would be easier if secure email were available.

Facilitators and Successes

Despite these challenges, UBHC staff reported success in developing and implementing their partnership. Many stakeholders reported that they viewed the center's very existence as a success. Indeed, as described in Chapter Four, the center has provided behavioral health services to a significant number of veterans and their families. Moreover, as described in Chapter Five, patients are extremely satisfied with the services they received.

"Champions" at both Northwell Health and the Northport VAMC facilitated the establishment of the UBHC. The CEO of Northwell Health has a long-standing commitment to helping veterans and their families (e.g., through the Rosen Center, through a program that ensured that deployed employees continued to earn as much as they did at home), and the UBHC was yet another way of expressing this commitment. The leadership of Northwell Health recognized the value of a center where both veterans and their families could receive colocated care that is directly coordinated with VA providers and was willing to implement such a facility with the understanding that it would be costly. Meanwhile, champions at the Northport VAMC were willing to pursue the UBHC even though they encountered substantial pushback from senior leaders at the Northport VAMC. The local champions similarly pressed forward with the VA Central Office and Office of General Counsel, which, although supportive, expressed concerns about how to make the center work, since regulations at the time were not conducive to this type of public-private collaboration.

An RWJF grant was a critical catalyst in the establishment of the center. Northwell Health received a $300,000 grant from the RWJF's Local Funding Partnerships initiative, a national program designed to support community-based projects that improve health care for vulnerable populations. External funding from the RWJF was a key catalyst that allowed the "champions" of the center to found the UBHC (using RWJF funds, as well as funding generated through Northwell Health fundraising efforts).

The strong working relationship between Northwell Health and Northport VAMC staff facilitated the center's establishment and implementation. Leadership and local staff from both organizations cited the collaborative working relationship as a factor that facilitated the initial founding of the center, as well as the later day-to-day operations and patient care. Northwell Health leadership reported that they had previously tried to establish a collaboration with the Northport VAMC without success, and the fact that it was successful this time may be in part because of the strong working relationships between collaborators from the different organizations and the high level of trust collaborators were able to achieve. Likewise, clinical staff from both organizations reported a high level of respect for staff from the other organization, which facilitates collaboration around patient care.

Another facilitator was the media attention that the UBHC received, which helped to advertise the center.

One marker of the success of the UBHC is the fact that the center now has a waiting list, indicating continued demand. Another marker is the reported close working relationship between on-site VA Clinic at Bay Shore and Feinberg Division providers, who reported that in many ways they have come together as a single working team. Providers on both sides praised the weekly team meetings as opportunities to learn about their patients and to enhance patient care for veterans and their families. UBHC providers also praised the flexibility of the staff participating in the collaboration.

The UBHC staff reported taking special pride in one achievement in particular: As one provider described it, "the healing that has occurred" as a result of being able to serve veterans' families through the provision of collaborative care.

Recommendations for Improving or Replicating the UBHC Model

We recommend the following for the current program and for other entities seeking to replicate the model in other locations. Many of these recommendations assume that a closer level of collaboration is desired; consequently, they should be implemented to the extent to which organizations want to and are able to integrate their practices.

1. Institutionalize and codify the practices that are working, such as:
    a. liaison role
    b. time to collaborate
    c. priority assignment of veterans to VA Clinic at Bay Shore (rather than other proximate VA facilities) if they have family members receiving care on the other side of the center.

The UBHC has established some strategies, policies, and procedures that enhance the collaborative effort. However, some of these practices have not been codified, so if there are changes in staffing, the practices might not be preserved. For instance, a member of the VA Clinic at Bay Shore staff is acting as a liaison between the organizations, playing an important coordination role and circumventing some of the information-sharing barriers identified above. However, this liaison role is not in her job description; she is not obligated to engage in the liaison activities, and if there is a change in staff, the center might no longer have someone serving in this capacity. Thus, we suggest that the liaison role be formalized to ensure that strong communication between organizations continues.

More broadly, the VA Clinic at Bay Shore should consider formally protecting the time that their providers spend collaborating, because this is time not spent in direct patient care or other administrative duties. The Feinberg Division has greater flexibility as a private organization, and thus has been able to formalize collaboration as a primary job responsibility and officially reduce the number of patient visits required of staff in order to carve out time for collaboration.

Similarly, while behavioral health intakes are coordinated through a central call center at the Northport VAMC, veterans are able to express a preference for a clinic, and if a veteran has a family member receiving care at the Feinberg Division of the UBHC, the veteran is prioritized for assignment to the VA Clinic at Bay Shore rather than other proximate VA facilities. This prioritization of shared family cases should be codified.

2. Facilitate easier and closer collaboration, by enhancing communication "infrastructure," including:
   a. integrated treatment plans
   b. shared patient treatment records or mutual access to records
   c. secure email.

Collaboration would be enhanced by use of integrated treatment plans that staff on both sides of the center contribute to and can readily access. Currently, staff verbally collaborate on treatment planning in their weekly meetings, and this is a key aspect of the UBHC approach. However, this planning is not documented in a shared treatment plan. Further, a shared treatment plan may further enhance the collaboration by helping the providers on the different sides of the center take a higher-level, systems-focused approach to treating the entire family unit (see, e.g., Celano, Smith, and Kaslow, 2010). The shared treatment plan would enhance coordination of treatment by explicating the higher-level goals the family is working toward. For these reasons, the UBHC is planning to implement a shared treatment plan (although one was not yet in place at the time of the evaluation). However, the current plan is for the integrated treatment plan to be a paper document that is stored on the Feinberg Division side of the center. While existence of a shared treatment plan would be a positive step toward enhancing the closeness of the collaboration, it would be ideal if the treatment plan could be stored electronically in such a way that providers from both sides of the UBHC could readily access it.

The collaboration could also be enhanced by providers on both sides of the center having easy access to each other's patient records, so that it is easier to track the care a patient is receiving from other providers.

It would also be helpful if providers could email each other securely; currently, they cannot include patient names in email communications, so communicating about a shared patient requires a phone call or an in-person consultation. As the center currently operates, communicating by phone or in person is a bit inconvenient but very feasible, since the sides are colocated and serve a relatively small number of shared cases, and the Bay Shore VA liaison acts as a point person facilitating communication. Although this approach works while the center is relatively small, it might not be scalable; if the center were larger, it would likely be more challenging to communicate with all the other providers in real time, and a liaison might not be able to relay communications among all providers in a timely manner.

Giving Feinberg Division staff Without Compensation (WOC) appointments at the VA, in which they serve as unpaid VA staff, would enable Feinberg Division providers to access VA treatment records and email communication systems, facilitating close communication among providers on the two sides of the UBHC. Indeed, other programs, such as Welcome Back Veterans, have used WOC appointments at the VA to facilitate seamless referrals from private organizations to the VA. WOC appointments would also enable the cofacilitation of groups, which some UBHC staff expressed interest in doing. However, WOC appointments also have some limitations and disadvantages. One obvious limitation is that a VA WOC appointment would only enable one-way access; Feinberg Division staff with a WOC could access VA electronic health record and communication systems, but the reverse would not be true. To facilitate communication in the other direction, Northwell Health would also have to give VA Clinic at Bay Shore staff a staff designation in the Northwell Health system, perhaps through the university affiliation system or some similar mechanism. However, even with mutual access, the treatment records would still be housed in two separate information systems, and there could be some logistical barriers to accessing the other organization's system. WOC appointments or their equivalent also present a burden to the staff involved and those who oversee them. For instance, Northwell Health staff who had VA WOC appointments would have to meet all the requirements of VA staff on an ongoing basis (e.g., mandated trainings), as well as all the requirements of Northwell Health staff, and managers overseeing these staff would have more people to track. For these reasons, a local VA administrator managing VA Clinic at Bay Shore behavioral health services felt that WOCs are not "worth it" for individuals who are not directly providing essential services to veterans, given that there are feasible work-arounds (i.e., in-person and phone communication). A possible solution could be for the organizations participating in the partnership to develop new policies or business arrangements that give staff at the other organizations staff privileges, but with less required oversight.

The organizations could also consider developing new platforms for secure electronic communication between different IT systems. The VA may broadly benefit from having its IT system be more private-sector facing. The VA is increasingly participating in public-private partnerships and may need to communicate with private-sector providers more often through its Community Care program, which facilitates veterans seeking care from private providers. As the VA looks toward solutions to enable this coordination, emerging technology can enable electronic record and data management systems to securely connect within health care settings. Enhanced communication infrastructure that facilitates less burdensome data collection, monitoring, and sharing is critical to supporting partnerships between the VA and private organizations, particularly when they are scaled beyond a single relatively small program.

3. Create a physical space that is conducive to collaboration and family friendly.

To be most effective, the clinic space should be organized in a manner that facilitates the coordination of care for clinical staff. In the current UBHC space, a shared conference room and kitchen promote close communication among staff in the collaborating organizations. This aspect of the program could be replicated by others who seek to implement the model, or they may wish to select other forms of shared, or neutral, spaces that allow for frequent and informal communication and relationship building, as well as more-formal clinical coordination.

Staff should also consider organizing the clinic in such a way that the collaboration and integration of services is readily apparent to patients. At present, the UBHC has two separate entrances for the Feinberg Division and the VA Clinic at Bay Shore sides of the center, with two separate reception desks and distinct signage and decor. If there were a single entrance, single reception, and uniform decor, this would communicate to patients that this is a truly collaborative center rather than two distinct entities. However, it is not clear that the appearance of greater unification is attractive to all patients. Some UBHC patients and the director of the Feinberg Division side reported that the fact that the center is not completely unified is appealing to a subset of patients. They reported that some patients like that the Feinberg Division side is not part of the VA, and that staff on the two sides of the UBHC can only communicate with patients' permission.

Regardless of the extent to which spaces are shared across organizations, there should be close communication regarding the establishment and construction of the physical space, so that expectations and specifications are clear from the start of the construction process.

As the UBHC and other sites seek to provide services to family members of veterans, including children, it will be important to ensure that these spaces appear not only veteran friendly but also family friendly. This may include appropriate waiting and service areas for children and families.

4. Ensure adequate capacity (i.e., staffing and space) to meet patient needs.

The UBHC may benefit from an expansion in both staffing and physical space, if patient interest in the center continues to grow. In particular, increased staff at the VA Clinic at Bay Shore would ensure that there is availability to serve veterans who have a family member receiving services on the Feinberg Division side of the UBHC.

In our interviews, providers from both sides of the UBHC noted that VA Clinic at Bay Shore providers do not have dedicated slots for patients who have family members receiving care on the Feinberg Division side and expressed that this might be helpful. However, local VA leadership pointed out that it is not practical to have dedicated slots for certain patients, because staff cannot anticipate how many referrals there will be for veterans participating in the collaboration, and staff cannot leave slots open and unused—they have a mandate to serve veterans in a timely manner. Instead, increasing the *overall* capacity of the VA Clinic at Bay Shore through increasing staff hours there (e.g., more full-time staff instead of part-time staff) would ensure that the VA Clinic at Bay Shore has adequate capacity to serve veterans participating in the collaboration, without affecting the capacity to serve veterans whose families do not receive care on the Feinberg Division side of the center. In addition, more on-site staff would allow the VA Clinic at Bay Shore to accept walk-in appointments; currently, it does not officially have a walk-in clinic as the Northport VAMC does, but it does accommodate veterans who walk in, in accordance with VA mandates. (The same could be said for the Feinberg Division, which also currently lacks capacity to officially accept walk-ins, although it does attempt to triage patients who walk in.) Finally, while the VA Clinic at Bay Shore currently has enough space to slightly increase staffing hours, it does not have adequate space to substantially expand its capacity to serve the veterans interested in receiving care there. The VA Clinic at Bay Shore currently has a waiting list for psychosocial services, indicating that interest currently exceeds capacity.

5. Provide a continuum of evidence-based services.

As more settings work to serve veterans and their families who experience behavioral health problems, it will be important not only to ensure the provision of evidence-based interventions but to also provide a continuum of services that includes prevention (e.g., psychoeducation and other programs) in addition to referrals to other types of support (e.g., financial/legal support, other family support services). Embracing a focus on prevention might serve to reduce the burden on veterans and their families before they are at the point of having clinically significant symptoms that require treatment. Incorporating these types of programs, however, may require different staff and different approaches to recruitment and service delivery. For both prevention and treatment services, community-based organizations and clinical settings should adopt a systematic approach for selecting, training, delivering, supervising, and monitoring fidelity of EBPs relevant to the population (e.g., exposure therapy for PTSD; empirically supported couples, parenting, and family interventions that have been adapted for military and veteran populations) (see Institute of Medicine, 2015). Systematic use of EBPs could ensure the effectiveness of treatment, provided that training is also systematic and that the interventions are delivered with fidelity. This could also serve to reduce the duration of treatment, facilitating the treatment of more patients, and potentially improve cost-benefit ratios for the clinic and society.

In choosing evidence-based approaches to care, organizations wishing to replicate the UBHC model may want to focus on time-limited (i.e., short-term) approaches and techniques or services that require lower-level (i.e., less expensive) staff, because the high intensity of services and high salary level of providers employed by the Feinberg Division may not be cost-effective or sustainable, particularly in larger settings. Use of time-limited approaches would increase the capacity to serve more patients, per the previous recommendation. Increased use of less expensive staff working to the full capacity of their licenses can serve to lower costs (see, e.g., Hussey et al., 2015). Indeed, RAND's 2015 Survey of VA Resources and Capabilities found that 68 percent of chiefs of staff across 111 VA sites reported that there were providers performing clinical activities that could be performed by providers with a lower level of training; this is a key issue that adversely affects the efficiency of providers and the system (Hussey et al., 2015).

6. Prioritize outcome monitoring and quality improvement for the center as a whole.

The UBHC and other similar centers should carefully and routinely reevaluate their battery of measures to choose measures that are least burdensome to patients and most helpful for informing clinical decisionmaking and outcome monitoring. For example, for children, using the CBCL alone may be limiting for capturing risk or outcomes in this population of children; thus, it may be useful to add measures of child depression and anxiety. In addition, some measures, such as the CBCL and BDI-II for adults, may be somewhat burdensome for routine collection given their length, so the center may wish to explore other options that make routine data collection more feasible. The center may also benefit from extending data collection to individuals who have completed care; follow-ups would inform how patients fare after they leave the center. Finally, we suggest that the center routinely implement brief risk screening for family "collateral" participants to guide services and referrals when needed.

To increase the integration and coordination of services, and to enable better tracking of patients outcomes over time, we recommend that the entire UBHC (both the VA Clinic at Bay Shore and Feinberg Division sides) implement the same set of patient-reported outcome measures, and we suggest a consistent and routine approach to data collection on both sides of the center. Doing so will not only inform patient care but also enable ongoing quality-improvement efforts across all partnering entities. For example, if families who received some care from both sides of the UBHC completed the same set of measures, it would facilitate setting and tracking higher-order, family system-level treatment goals. Consistent measurement across the entire UBHC would also facilitate program monitoring and evaluation.

Conclusions

Our analyses found that, overall, the UBHC has succeeded in implementing a promising public-private partnership model for providing behavioral health care for veterans and their families in the same facility: Providers coordinated their efforts to provide a higher quality of care, the center ramped up to deliver a wide array of therapeutic services for a large number of patients in a relatively short period, patients reported being happy with the services they received, and their symptoms and functioning improved significantly over time.

The UBHC provision of colocated and coordinated care has the potential to address barriers to care. While veterans are eligible for VA services, most of their families are not eligible, leading different members of families to seek care in different settings, with no easy way to exchange information and coordinate care between VA providers and family members' providers (see Pedersen et al., 2015, for a review). The

UBHC addresses this barrier by providing care that is colocated and coordinated.

Further, the UBHC provides care that is sensitive to the special needs of veterans' families. Family members we spoke with expressed that the UBHC plays a vital role in their community, citing that, in their experience, providers not affiliated with the VA are not sensitive to the impact of PTSD and other special issues facing veterans' families. Family members we interviewed saw the UBHC as a unique place where military families could receive care and be understood. UBHC staff and patients alike touted the advantages of coordinated care in which the different providers treating a family are in close communication with one another; all interviewees felt that it greatly improved the quality of care that all family members received. Patients expressed high levels of satisfaction with the care they received, according to the qualitative RAND focus groups and the quantitative surveys administered by the Feinberg Division to its patients.

The service utilization and outcome data available also provide early evidence of successful program implementation. Service utilization data from both sides of the UBHC indicated that, for a new program in a small facility, a relatively large volume of care was delivered. In focus group discussions, patients reported a high level of satisfaction with the care they received; however, the interviews were limited in that they consisted of just one group of entirely male veterans and another of entirely female family members; child patients and nonpatient collaterals were not included. The outcome data from the Feinberg Division side of the UBHC provide evidence that the center is helping patients as intended: Both adult and child patients experienced statistically and clinically significant improvements in almost all kinds of behavioral health symptomatology and measures of functioning evaluated. However, it should be noted that the outcome data are limited by the absence of a control group with which we can compare patients, and patients do tend to get better over time even without care. Consequently, while we know that patients got better, we do not know for certain whether their improvements are greater than they would have experienced had they not received care at the Feinberg Division of the UBHC. Further, clinicians had some discretion in choosing outcome measures appropriate for a given patient, so this could have introduced some bias in the available data. Finally, outcome data are not available for patients receiving services on the VA Clinic at Bay Shore side of the center.

Although the model has been successfully implemented with strong preliminary outcomes, there are still areas that could be improved as the UBHC continues to grow and develop. While staff and patients were happy with the collaborative relationships between providers, collaboration could still be closer than it currently is. The staff have to regularly circumvent various challenges to collaboration, including a lack of secure email between Feinberg Division and VA Clinic at Bay Shore providers that necessitates that all information sharing be via phone or in person, lack of shared patient health records, and a lack of a shared treatment plan for families receiving care on both sides of the center. We recommend that this center and others seeking to replicate the model work toward reducing information-sharing barriers and, if desired, find ways to facilitate closer collaboration. We further recommend that the UBHC institutionalize and codify the practices that are working, including a VA liaison role, time for collaboration, and the VA Clinic at Bay Shore's prioritization of veterans who have family members receiving care at the UBHC.

Other partnerships between local VAMCs and private health systems that want to accomplish similar objectives can learn from the UBHC launch and implementation. In addition to the issues related to barriers to collaboration and the lack of codified practices, there were some barriers to establishing the center that other programs may be able to circumvent. Building the center was a complicated process, but many of the barriers the UBHC faced could potentially be avoided by having close communication between the private organization and appropriate VA staff through all phases of establishing the center, with all key players at the table from the start of the process. Another potential barrier for other potential partnerships is how expensive the program was to launch and implement. However, initial expenses could be greatly reduced by utilizing an existing facility rather than building a new one. Further, ongoing expenses could be reduced by billing patients from the start and potentially using less expensive staff (e.g., less psychiatry, greater use of interns) and providing less expensive care (e.g., less individual therapy and more groups; however, this may not be feasible for small centers).

The UBHC was the first center of its kind; it broke new ground by using a public-private partnership model to provide colocated, coordinated care to veterans and their families. Despite some challenges, our evaluation suggests that, overall, the model has been successfully implemented by the UBHC and has great potential to be helpful to the veterans' families it serves.

Abbreviations

ARC	attachment, self-regulation, and competency
BAI	Beck Anxiety Inventory
BDI-II	Beck Depression Inventory II
CBCL	Child Behavior Checklist
CBOC	community-based outpatient clinic
CBT	cognitive-behavioral therapy
CPT	cognitive processing therapy
DAS	Dyadic Adjustment Scale
DoD	U.S. Department of Defense
EBP	evidence-based practice
EFT	emotionally focused therapy
FAD	Family Assessment Device
IT	information technology
LEC	Life Events Checklist
MOU	memorandum of understanding
NYS	New York state
PCL	Posttraumatic Stress Disorder Checklist
PE	prolonged exposure
PTSD	posttraumatic stress disorder
Q-LES-Q–SF	Quality of Life Enjoyment and Satisfaction Questionnaire–Short Form

RWJF	Robert Wood Johnson Foundation
SD	standard deviation
SE	standard error
TBI	traumatic brain injury
UBHC	Unified Behavioral Health Center
VA	Department of Veterans Affairs
VAMC	Veterans Affairs Medical Center
VHA	Veterans Health Administration
VISN	Veterans Integrated Service Network
WOC	Without Compensation
YSR	Youth Self Report

References

Achenbach, T., *Manual for the Youth Self-Report and 1991 Profile*, Burlington: Department of Psychiatry, University of Vermont, 1991.

Achenbach, T. M., and L. A. Rescorla, *Manual for the ASEBA School-Age Forms and Profiles*, Burlington: Research Center for Children, Youth, and Families, University of Vermont, 2001.

Assistant Deputy Under Secretary for Health for Policy and Planning, "VISN Performance Measurement and Systems Monitoring," in *Vision for Change: A Plan to Restructure the Veterans Health Administration*, Washington, D.C., 1995, pp. 61–74. As of July 21, 2016:
http://www.va.gov/HEALTHPOLICYPLANNING/VISION/5CHAP4.pdf

Beck, A. T., N. Epstein, G. Brown, and R. A. Steer, "An Inventory for Measuring Clinical Anxiety: Psychometric Properties," *Journal of Consulting and Clinical Psychology*, Vol. 56, No. 6, 1988, pp. 893–897.

Beck, A. T., and R. A. Steer, *Beck Anxiety Inventory Manual*, San Antonio, Tex.: Psychological Corporation, 1993.

Beck, A. T., R. A. Steer, and G. K. Brown, *Manual for the Beck Depression Inventory–II*, San Antonio, Tex.: Psychological Corporation, 1996.

Bihum, J. T., M. Z. Wamboldt, L. A. Gavin, and F. S. Wamboldt, "Can the Family Assessment Device (FAD) Be Used with School Aged Children?" *Family Process*, Vol. 41, No. 4, 2002, pp. 723–731.

Blevins, C. A., F. W. Weathers, M. T. Davis, T. K. Witte, and J. L. Domino, "The Posttraumatic Stress Disorder Checklist for DSM-5 (PCL-5): Development and Initial Psychometric Evaluation," *Journal of Traumatic Stress*, Vol. 28, No. 6, 2015, pp. 489–498.

Bray, R. M., and L. L. Hourani, "Substance Use Trends Among Active Duty Military Personnel: Findings from the United States Department of Defense Health Related Behavior Surveys, 1980–2005," *Addiction*, Vol. 102, No. 7, 2007, pp. 1092–1101.

Carey, Michael P., Ilana P. Spector, Larry J. Lantinga, and Dennis J. Krauss, "Reliability of the Dyadic Adjustment Scale," *Psychological Assessment*, Vol. 5, No. 2, 1993, pp. 238–240.

Celano, Marianne P., Chaundrissa Oyeshiku Smith, and Nadine J. Kaslow, "A Competency-Based Approach to Couple and Family Therapy Supervision," *Psychotherapy: Theory, Research, Practice, Training*, Vol. 47, No. 1, 2010, pp. 35–44.

Cohen, P. M., "Locke Martial Adjustment Scale and the Dyadic Adjustment Scale," *American Journal of Family Therapy*, Vol. 13, 1985, pp. 66–71.

DoD—*See* U.S. Department of Defense.

Donabedian, A., "Evaluating the Quality of Medical Care," *Milbank Memorial Fund Quarterly*, Vol. 44, No. 3, 1966, pp. 166–206.

———, "Methods for Deriving Criteria for Assessing the Quality of Medical Care," *Medical Care Review*, Vol. 37, No. 7, 1980, pp. 653–698.

Dozois, David J. A., Keith S. Dobson, and Jaime L. Ahnberg, "A Psychometric Evaluation of the Beck Depression Inventory–II," *Psychological Assessment*, Vol. 10, No. 2, 1998, pp. 83–89.

Eaton, K. M., C. W. Hoge, S. C. Messer, A. A. Whitt, O. A. Cabrera, D. McGurk, A. Cox, and C. A. Castro, "Prevalence of Mental Health Problems, Treatment Need, and Barriers to Care Among Primary Care-Seeking Spouses of Military Service Members Involved in Iraq and Afghanistan Deployments," *Military Medicine*, Vol. 173, No. 11, 2008, pp. 1051–1056.

Ebesutani, C., A. Bernstein, J. I. Martinez, B. F. Chorpita, and J. R. Weisz, "The Youth Self Report: Applicability and Validity Across Younger and Older Youths," *Journal of Clinical Child and Adolescent Psychology*, Vol. 40, No. 2, 2011, pp. 338–346.

Endicott, J., J. Nee, W. Harrison, and R. Blumenthal, "Quality of Life Enjoyment and Satisfaction Questionnaire: A New Measure," *Psychopharmacology Bulletin*, Vol. 29, No. 2, 1993, pp. 321–326.

Engel, C. C., K. C. Hyams, and K. Scott, "Managing Future Gulf War Syndromes: International Lessons and New Models of Care," *Philosophical Transactions of the Royal Society of London B: Biological Sciences*, Vol. 361, No. 1468, 2006, pp. 707–720.

Epstein, N. B., L. M. Baldwin, and D. S. Bishop, "The McMaster Family Assessment Device," *Journal of Marital and Family Therapy*, Vol. 9, No. 2, 1983, pp. 171–180.

Farmer, Carrie, Terry L. Schell, Lisa H. Jaycox, Terri Tanielian, and Glenda Wrenn, "Qualitative Needs Assessment of New York State Veterans," in Terry L. Schell and Terri Tanielian, eds., *A Needs Assessment of New York State Veterans: Final Report to the New York State Health Foundation*, Santa Monica, Calif.: RAND Corporation, TR-920-NYSHF, 2011, pp. 5–22. As of July 18, 2016: http://www.rand.org/pubs/technical_reports/TR920.html

Flake, E. M., B. E. Davis, P. L. Johnson, and L. S. Middleton, "The Psychosocial Effects of Deployment on Military Children," *Journal of Developmental and Behavioral Pediatrics*, Vol. 30, No. 4, 2009, pp. 271–278.

Fydrich, T., D. Dowdall, and D. L. Chambless, "Reliability and Validity of the Beck Anxiety Inventory," *Journal of Anxiety Disorders*, Vol. 6, No. 1, 1992, pp. 55–61.

Gewirtz, A. H., M. A. Polusny, D. S. DeGarmo, A. Khaylis, and C. R. Erbes, "Posttraumatic Stress Symptoms Among National Guard Soldiers Deployed to Iraq: Associations with Parenting Behaviors and Couple Adjustment," *Journal of Consulting in Clinical Psychology*, Vol. 78, No. 5, 2010, pp. 599–610.

Gorman, Gregory H., Matilda Eide, and Elizabeth Hisle-Gorman, "Wartime Military Deployment and Increased Pediatric Mental and Behavioral Health Complaints," *Pediatrics*, November 8, 2010.

Gorman, L. A., A. J. Blow, B. D. Ames, and P. L. Reed, "National Guard Families After Combat: Mental Health, Use of Mental Health Services, and Perceived Treatment Barriers," *Psychiatric Services*, Vol. 62, No. 1, January 2011, pp. 28–34.

Graham, J. M., Y. J. Liu, and J. L. Jeziorski, "The Dyadic Adjustment Scale: A Reliability Generalization Meta-Analysis," *Journal of Marriage and Family*, Vol. 68, 2006, pp. 701–717.

Hansen, N. B., M. J. Lambert, and E. M. Forman, "The Psychotherapy Dose-Response Effect and Its Implications for Treatment Delivery Services," *Clinical Psychology: Science and Practice*, Vol. 9, No. 3, 2002, pp. 329–343.

Hoge, Charles W., Carl A. Castro, Stephen C. Messer, Dennis McGurk, Dave I. Cotting, and Robert L. Koffman, "Combat Duty in Iraq and Afghanistan, Mental Health Problems, and Barriers to Care," *New England Journal of Medicine*, Vol. 351, No. 1, 2004, pp. 13–22.

Hussey, Peter S., Jeanne S. Ringel, Sangeeta Ahluwalia, Rebecca Anhang Price, Christine Buttorff, Thomas W. Concannon, Susan L. Lovejoy, Grant R. Martsolf, Robert S. Rudin, Dana Schultz, Elizabeth M. Sloss, Katherine E. Watkins, Daniel Waxman, Melissa Bauman, Brian Briscombe, James R. Broyles, Rachel M. Burns, Emily K. Chen, Amy Soo Jin DeSantis, Liisa Ecola, Shira H. Fischer, Mark W. Friedberg, Courtney A. Gidengil, Paul B. Ginsburg, Timothy Gulden, Carlos Ignacio Gutierrez, Samuel Hirshman, Christina Y. Huang, Ryan Kandrack, Amii Kress, Kristin J. Leuschner, Sarah MacCarthy, Ervant J. Maksabedian, Sean Mann, Luke Joseph Matthews, Linnea Warren May, Nishtha Mishra, Lisa Miyashiro, Ashley N. Muchow, Jason Nelson, Diana Naranjo, Claire E. O'Hanlon, Francesca Pillemer, Zachary Predmore, Rachel Ross, Teague Ruder, Carolyn M. Rutter, Lori Uscher-Pines, Mary E. Vaiana, Joseph V. Vesely, Susan D. Hosek, and Carrie M. Farmer, *Resources and Capabilities of the Department of Veterans Affairs to Provide Timely and Accessible Care to Veterans*, Santa Monica, Calif.: RAND Corporation, RR-1165/2-VA, 2015. As of July 18, 2016: http://www.rand.org/pubs/research_reports/RR1165z2.html

Institute of Medicine, *Psychosocial Interventions for Mental and Substance Use Disorders: A Framework for Establishing Evidence-Based Standards*, Washington, D.C.: The National Academies Press, 2015.

Izutsu, Takashi, Atsuro Tsutsumi, Akramul Islam, A. H. Mohammad Firoz, Susumu Wakai, and Hiroshi Kurita, "Reliability and Validity of the Youth Self-Report," Bangladesh version, *International Journal of Methods in Psychiatric Research*, Vol. 14, No. 4, 2005, pp. 212–220.

Jacobson, N. S., and W. C. Follette, "Clinical Significance of Improvement Resulting from Two Behavioral Marital Therapy Components," *Behavior Therapy*, Vol. 16, No. 3, 1985, pp. 249–262.

Johnson, S. M., and L. S. Greenberg, "Emotionally Focused Couples Therapy: An Outcome Study," *Journal of Marital and Family Therapy*, Vol. 11, No. 3, 1985, pp. 313–317.

Jordan, B. K., C. R. Marmar, J. A. Fairbank, W. E. Schlenger, R. A. Kulka, R. L. Hough, and D. S. Weiss, "Problems in Families of Male Vietnam Veterans with Posttraumatic Stress Disorder," *Journal of Consulting and Clinical Psychology*, Vol. 60, No. 6, 1992, pp. 916–926.

Kabacoff, Robert I., Ivan W. Miller, Duane S. Bishop, Nathan B. Epstein, and Gabor I. Keitner, "A Psychometric Study of the McMaster Family Assessment Device in Psychiatric, Medical, and Nonclinical Samples," *Journal of Family Psychology*, Vol. 3, No. 4, 1990, pp. 431–439.

Katon, W., C. Rutter, E. J. Ludman, M. Von Korff, E. Lin, G. Simon, T. Bush, E. Walker, and J. Unützer, "A Randomized Trial of Relapse Prevention of Depression in Primary Care," *Archives of General Psychiatry*, Vol. 58, No. 3, 2000, pp. 241–247.

Lester, Patricia, Kris Peterson, James Reeves, Larry Knauss, Dorie Glover, Catherine Mogil, Naihua Duan, William Saltzman, Robert Pynoos, Katherine Wilt, and William Beardslee, "The Long War and Parental Combat Deployment: Effects on Military Children and At-Home Spouses," *Journal of the American Academy of Child and Adolescent Psychiatry*, Vol. 49, No. 4, 2010, pp. 310–320.

Liu, P., L. Wang, C. Cao, R. Wang, J. Zhang, B. Zhang, Q. Wu, H. Zhang, G. Fan, and J. D. Elhai, "The Underlying Dimensions of DSM-5 Posttraumatic Stress Disorder Symptoms in an Epidemiological Sample of Chinese Earthquake Survivors," *Journal of Anxiety Disorders*, Vol. 28, No. 4, 2014, pp. 345–351.

Mansfield, Alyssa J., Jay S. Kaufman, Charles C. Engel, and Bradley N. Gaynes, "Deployment and Mental Health Diagnoses Among Children of US Army Personnel," *Archives of Pediatric and Adolescent Medicine*, Vol. 165, No. 11, 2011, pp. 999–1005.

Mansfield, Alyssa J., Jay S. Kaufman, Stephen W. Marshall, Bradley N. Gaynes, Joseph P. Morrissey, and Charles C. Engel, "Deployment and the Use of Mental Health Services Among U.S. Army Wives," *New England Journal of Medicine*, Vol. 362, No. 2, 2010, pp. 101–109.

McFarlane, A. C., "Military Deployment: The Impact on Children and Family Adjustment and the Need for Care," *Current Opinion in Psychiatry*, Vol. 22, No. 4, 2009, pp. 369–373.

McGuire, Marsden, Paula Schnurr, and Tracey L. Smith, "Prolonged Exposure: A First-Line Treatment for PTSD," web page, U.S. Department of Veterans Affairs, January 15, 2015. As of July 20, 2016:
http://www.blogs.va.gov/VAntage/16793/prolonged-exposure-a-first-line-treatment-for-ptsd/

Meadows, Sarah O., Terri Tanielian, and Benjamin R. Karney, *The Deployment Life Study: Longitudinal Analysis of Military Families Across the Deployment Cycle*, Santa Monica, Calif.: RAND Corporation, RR-1388-A/OSD, 2016. As of July 18, 2016:
http://www.rand.org/pubs/research_reports/RR1388.html

Mick, Eric, Stephen V. Faraone, Thomas Spencer, Huabin F. Zhang, and Joseph Biederman, "Assessing the Validity of the Quality of Life Enjoyment and Satisfaction Questionnaire Short Form in Adults with ADHD," *Journal of Attention Disorders*, Vol. 11, No. 4, 2008, pp. 504–509.

Miklowitz, D. J., M. W. Otto, E. Frank, N. A. Reilly-Harrington, S. R. Wisniewski, J. N. Kogan, A. A. Nierenberg, J. R. Calabrese, L. B. Marangell, L. Gyulai, M. Araga, J. M. Gonzalez, E. R. Shirley, M. E. Thase, and G. S. Sachs, "Psychosocial Treatments for Bipolar Depression: A 1-Year Randomized Trial from the Systematic Treatment Enhancement Program," *Archives of General Psychiatry*, Vol. 64, No. 4, 2007, pp. 419–426.

Miller, Ivan W., Nathan B. Epstein, Duane S. Bishop, and Gabor I. Keitner, "The McMaster Family Assessment Device: Reliability and Validity," *Journal of Marital and Family Therapy*, Vol. 11, No. 4, 1985, pp. 345–356.

Miranda, J., N. Duan, C. Sherbourne, M. Schoenbaum, I. Lagomasino, M. Jackson-Triche, and K. B. Wells, "Improving Care for Minorities: Can Quality Improvement Interventions Improve Care and Outcomes for Depressed Minorities? Results of a Randomized, Controlled Trial," *Health Services Research*, Vol. 38, No. 2, 2003, pp. 613–630.

Nakamura, Brad J., Chad Ebesutani, Adam Bernstein, and Bruce F. Chorpita, "A Psychometric Analysis of the Child Behavior Checklist DSM-Oriented Scales," *Journal of Psychopathology and Behavioral Assessment*, Vol. 31, No. 3, 2009, pp. 178–189.

National Center for Veterans Analysis and Statistics, U.S. Department of Veterans Affairs, "Veteran Population," web page, undated. As of July 18, 2016: http://www.va.gov/vetdata/Veteran_Population.asp

Norman, G. R., J. A. Sloan, and K. W. Wyrwich, "Interpretation of Changes in Health-Related Quality of Life: The Remarkable Universality of Half a Standard Deviation," *Medical Care*, Vol. 5, 2003, pp. 582–592.

Office of Policy and Planning, U.S. Department of Veterans Affairs, *Veterans Policy Research Agenda: Fiscal Year 2015*, Washington, D.C., 2014.

Office of the Press Secretary, White House, "Executive Order—Improving Access to Mental Health Services for Veterans, Service Members, and Military Families," Washington, D.C., August 31, 2012.

Office of Warrior and Family Support, Office of the Chairman of the Joint Chiefs of Staff, *White Paper: Expanding Public-Private Partnerships*, Washington, D.C., 2013.

Osman, Augustine, Beverly A. Kopper, Frank Barrios, Peter M. Gutierrez, and Courtney L. Bagge, "Reliability and Validity of the Beck Depression Inventory–II with Adolescent Psychiatric Inpatients," *Psychological Assessment*, Vol. 16, No. 2, 2004, pp. 120–132.

Pedersen, Eric R., Nicole K. Eberhart, Kayla M. Williams, Terri Tanielian, Caroline Batka, and Deborah M. Scharf, *Public-Private Partnerships for Providing Behavioral Health Care to Veterans and Their Families: What Do We Know, What Do We Need to Learn, and What Do We Need to Do?* Santa Monica, Calif.: RAND Corporation, RR-994-NYSHF/MTF, 2015. As of July 18, 2016: http://www.rand.org/pubs/research_reports/RR994.html

Pietrzak, R. H., D. C. Johnson, M. B. Goldstein, J. C. Malley, and S. M. Southwick, "Perceived Stigma and Barriers to Mental Health Care Utilization Among OEF-OIF Veterans," *Psychiatric Services*, Vol. 60, No. 8, August 2009, pp. 1118–1122.

Pietrzak, R. H., J. Tsai, C. Armour, N. Mota, I. Harpaz-Rotem, and S. M. Southwick, "Functional Significance of a Novel 7-Factor Model of DSM-5 PTSD Symptoms: Results from the National Health and Resilience in Veterans Study," *Journal of Affective Disorders*, Vol. 174, 2015, pp. 522–526.

Ramchand, Rajeev, Terri Tanielian, Michael P. Fisher, Christine Anne Vaughan, Thomas E. Trail, Caroline Batka, Phoenix Voorhies, Michael Robbins, Eric Robinson, and Bonnie Ghosh-Dastidar, *Hidden Heroes: America's Military Caregivers*, Santa Monica, Calif.: RAND Corporation, RR-499-TEDF, 2014. As of July 18, 2016:
http://www.rand.org/pubs/research_reports/RR499.html

Ritsner, M., R. Kurs, A. Gibel, Y. Ratner, and J. Endicott, "Validity of an Abbreviated Quality of Life Enjoyment and Satisfaction Questionnaire (Q-LES-Q-18) for Schizophrenia, Schizoaffective, and Mood Disorder Patients," *Quality of Life Research*, Vol. 14, No. 7, 2005, pp. 1693–1703.

Riviere, L. A., J. C. Merrill, J. L. Thomas, J. E. Wilk, and P. D. Bliese, "2003–2009 Marital Functioning Trends Among U.S. Enlisted Soldiers Following Combat Deployments," *Military Medicine*, Vol. 177, No. 10, 2012, pp. 1169–1177.

North Shore-LIJ Health System, *Unified Behavioral Health Center for Military Veterans and Their Families*, semiannual report, Great Neck, N.Y., 2013.

———, *Unified Behavioral Health Center for Military Veterans and Their Families*, annual report, Great Neck, N.Y., 2014.

———, *Unified Behavioral Health Center for Military Veterans and Their Families*, final narrative report, Great Neck, N.Y., 2015.

Sayers, S. L., V. A. Farrow, J. Ross, and D. W. Oslin, "Family Problems Among Recently Returned Military Veterans Referred for a Mental Health Evaluation," *Journal of Clinical Psychiatry*, Vol. 70, No. 2, 2009, pp. 163–170.

Schell, Terry L., and Grant N. Marshall, "Survey of Individuals Previously Deployed for OEF/OIF," in Terri Tanielian and Lisa H. Jaycox, eds., *Invisible Wounds of War: Psychological and Cognitive Injuries, Their Consequences, and Services to Assist Recovery*, Santa Monica, Calif.: RAND Corporation, MG-720-CCF, 2008, pp. 87–115. As of July 18, 2016:
http://www.rand.org/pubs/monographs/MG720.html

Schell, Terry L., and Terri Tanielian, eds., *A Needs Assessment of New York State Veterans: Final Report to the New York State Health Foundation*, Santa Monica, Calif.: RAND Corporation, TR-920-NYSHF, 2011. As of April 9, 2015:
http://www.rand.org/pubs/technical_reports/TR920.html

Schultz, M., M. E. Glickman, and S. V. Eisen, "Predictors of Decline in Overall Mental Health, PTSD and Alcohol Use in OEF/OIF Veterans," *Comprehensive Psychiatry*, Vol. 55, 2014, pp. 1654–1664.

Seal, K. H., G. Cohen, A. Waldrop, B. E. Cohen, S. Maguen, and L. Ren, "Substance Use Disorders in Iraq and Afghanistan Veterans in VA Healthcare, 2001–2010: Implications for Screening, Diagnosis and Treatment," *Drug and Alcohol Dependence*, Vol. 116, Nos. 1–3, July 2011, pp. 93–101.

Sharpley, C. F., and D. G. Cross, "A Psychometric Evaluation of the Spanier Dyadic Adjustment Scale," *Journal of Marriage and Family*, Vol. 44, No. 3, 1982, pp. 739–741.

Spanier, Graham B., "Measuring Dyadic Adjustment: New Scales for Assessing the Quality of Marriage and Similar Dyads," *Journal of Marriage and the Family*, Vol. 38, No. 1, 1976, pp. 15–28.

Stevanovic, D., "Quality of Life Enjoyment and Satisfaction Questionnaire—Short Form for Quality of Life Assessments in Clinical Practice: A Psychometric Study," *Journal of Psychiatric and Mental Health Nursing*, Vol. 18, No. 8, 2011, pp. 744–750.

Stulz, N., and W. Lutz, "Multidimensional Patterns of Change in Outpatient Psychotherapy: The Phase Model Revisited," *Journal of Clinical Psychology*, Vol. 63, No. 9, 2007, pp. 817–833.

Suter, E., N. D. Oelke, C. E. Adair, and G. D. Armitage, "Ten Key Principles for Successful Health Systems Integration," *Healthcare Quarterly*, 2009, special issue, pp. 16–23.

Tanielian, Terri, Coreen Farris, Caroline Batka, Carrie M. Farmer, Eric Robinson, Charles C. Engel, Michael Robbins, and Lisa H. Jaycox, *Ready to Serve: Community Based Provider Capacity to Deliver Culturally Competent, Quality Mental Health Care to Veterans and Their Families*, Santa Monica, Calif.: RAND Corporation, RR-806-UNHF, 2014. As of July 18, 2016:
http://www.rand.org/pubs/research_reports/RR806.html

Uher, R., O. Mors, M. Rietschel, A. Rajewska-Rager, A. Petrovic, A. Zobel, N. Henigsberg, J. Mendlewicz, K. J. Aitchison, A. Farmer, and P. McGuffin, "Early and Delayed Onset of Response to Antidepressants in Individual Trajectories of Change During Treatment of Major Depression: A Secondary Analysis of Data from the Genome-Based Therapeutic Drugs for Depression (GENDEP) Study," *The Journal of Clinical Psychiatry*, Vol. 72, No. 11, 2011, pp. 1478–1484.

U.S. Department of Defense, *Demographics 2010: Profile of the Military Community*, Washington, D.C., 2010. As of July 18, 2016:
http://download.militaryonesource.mil/12038/MOS/Reports/2010_Demographics_Report.pdf

U.S. Department of Defense, U.S. Department of Veterans Affairs, and U.S. Department of Health and Human Services, *Interagency Task Force on Military and Veterans Mental Health: 2013 Interim Report*, Washington, D.C., 2013.

U.S. Department of Veterans Affairs, "Mental Health Clinical Practice Guidelines," web page, undated. As of July 21, 2016:
http://www.healthquality.va.gov/HEALTHQUALITY/guidelines/MH/index.asp

VA—*See* U.S. Department of Veterans Affairs.

Vaughan, Christine Anne, Terry L. Schell, Lisa H. Jaycox, Grant N. Marshall, and Terri Tanielian, "Quantitative Needs Assessment of New York State Veterans and Their Spouses," in Terry L. Schell and Terri Tanielian, eds., *A Needs Assessment of New York State Veterans: Final Report to the New York State Health Foundation*, Santa Monica, Calif.: RAND Corporation, TR-920-NYSHF, 2011, pp. 23–52. As of April 9, 2015:
http://www.rand.org/pubs/technical_reports/TR920.html

Watkins, Katherine E., Harold Alan Pincus, Brad Smith, Susan M. Paddock, Thomas E. Mannle, Abigail Woodroffe, Jake Solomon, Melony E. Sorbero, Carrie M. Farmer, Kimberly A. Hepner, David M. Adamson, Lanna Forrest, and Catherine Call, *Veterans Health Administration Mental Health Program Evaluation: Capstone Report*, Santa Monica, Calif.: RAND Corporation, TR-956-VHA, 2011. As of July 21, 2016:
http://www.rand.org/pubs/technical_reports/TR956.html

Weathers, F. W., B. T. Litz, T. M. Keane, P. A. Palmieri, B. P. Marx, and P. P. Schnurr, "PTSD Checklist for DSM-5 (PCL-5)," Washington, D.C.: National Center for PTSD, 2013. As of July 18, 2016:
http://www.ptsd.va.gov/professional/assessment/adult-sr/ptsd-checklist.asp